YALE STUDIES IN ENGLISH

Benjamin Christie Nangle, Editor

VOLUME 159

GEORGE ELIOT'S

SCENES OF CLERICAL LIFE

by Thomas A. Noble

NEW HAVEN AND LONDON
YALE UNIVERSITY PRESS
1965

Copyright © 1965 by Yale University.
Designed by Crimilda Pontes,
set in Garamond type,
and printed in the United States of America by
the Carl Purington Rollins Printing-Office
of the Yale University Press.
Distributed in Canada by McGill University Press.

Library of Congress catalog card number: 65–19755

FOR MY MOTHER AND FATHER

PREFACE

This study deals with George Eliot's art and thought in her first work of fiction. In the hundred-odd years since its publication, *Scenes of Clerical Life* has received very little critical attention. The most generous critics have given it a few casual pages; often, it is mentioned only in passing. While it is perhaps not surprising that this work should have been overshadowed by the greater achievement of her full-length novels, *Scenes of Clerical Life* deserves and rewards close consideration as the first production of a major novelist. In these stories we see emerging the literary and philosophical principles that made George Eliot's work a significant departure in the history of English fiction.

The plan of this book will be apparent from a glance at the table of contents. The first chapter is mainly descriptive, being an account of the composition, publication, and reception of the work. I have indicated the extent to which the stories were drawn from life, and have discussed George Eliot's use of factual material. The material dealt with is familiar, but it is hoped that the subsequent discussion will be of more interest and value for being placed in the perspective of literary history. Chapter 2 deals with the theory of fiction upon which *Scenes of Clerical Life* is based. George Eliot's critical articles in the *Westminster Review,* from which this theory may be inferred, are here used to furnish a background for the discussion of her correspondence with her publisher during the writing of the *Scenes*. In Chapter 3 the work is considered as an expression of George Eliot's moral philosophy. Chapter 4 deals with various aspects of her narrative technique; I have treated each story separately as an experiment in the handling of the novelist's materials, concentrating upon the particular elements of narrative art with which George Eliot was mainly concerned in each case: humor and pathos in "Amos Barton," romantic characterization and setting in "Mr. Gilfil's Love Story," and the creation of a realistic social milieu in "Janet's Repentance." In the Afterword I have suggested ways (other than those considered in Chapters 3 and 4) in which *Scenes of Clerical Life* foreshadows George Eliot's subsequent work. Examination of the manuscript of *Scenes of Clerical Life* has revealed several significant revisions, and these I have dealt with wherever most relevant to the discussion.

The present book was presented, in a slightly different form, to the faculty of the Graduate School of Yale University as a doctoral dissertation. For invaluable advice during the writing of the dissertation, I am indebted to Professor Gordon S. Haight, in whose seminar on the English novel I first became interested in George Eliot. Professor Haight's patience and scholarly guidance have been matched only by his personal kindness to me, and I am happy to record my thanks to him as both teacher and friend. I should also like to express my appreciation for their generous encouragement to Dean William C. DeVane, Professor Richard L. Purdy, and Mrs. Basil Henning, who read this book in its earlier form. Finally, I am grateful to the members of the committee on Yale Studies in English who read my manuscript and judged it worthy of publication.

THOMAS A. NOBLE

New Haven, Connecticut
November 1964

NOTE: All quotations from the published version of *Scenes of Clerical Life* are from the first edition (2 vols., Edinburgh and London, 1858). I am grateful to Mrs. E. Carrington Ouvry, George Henry Lewes' granddaughter, for permission to quote unpublished material from the manuscript, and to the owners of the manuscript, the Pierpont Morgan Library, for kindly giving me access to it.

CONTENTS

1. THE WORK AND ITS RECEPTION

In December 1857, George Eliot wrote in her journal, under the title "How I Came to Write Fiction," an account of the genesis of her first story:

> September 1856 made a new era in my life, for it was then I began to write Fiction. It had always been a vague dream of mine that some time or other I might write a novel, and my shadowy conception of what the novel was to be, varied, of course, from each epoch of my life to another. But I never went farther towards the actual writing . . . than an introductory chapter describing a Staffordshire village and the life of the neighbouring farm houses, and as the years passed on I lost any hope that I should ever be able to write a novel, just as I desponded about everything else in my future life.[1]

The fragment happened to be among the papers George Eliot took with her to Germany when she and George Henry Lewes first left England together in 1854, and one evening in Berlin she read it

---

1. Gordon S. Haight, ed. *The George Eliot Letters* (7 vols. New Haven, 1954–55), 2, 406; referred to hereafter in text and notes as *Letters*.

to him. "He was struck with it as a bit of concrete description,"
George Eliot writes.

> He began to think that I might as well try, some time, what
> I could do in fiction, and by and bye when we came back to
> England and I had greater success than he had ever expected
> in other kinds of writing, his impression that it was worth
> while to see how far my mental power would go towards the
> production of a novel, was strengthened. He began to say
> very positively, "You must try and write a story," and when
> we were at Tenby[2] he urged me to begin at once. I deferred
> it, however, after my usual fashion, with work that does not
> present itself as an absolute duty. But one morning as I was
> lying in bed, thinking what should be the subject of my first
> story, my thoughts merged themselves into a dreamy doze,
> and I imagined myself writing a story of which the title was
> —"The Sad Fortunes of the Reverend Amos Barton." I was
> soon wide awake again, and told G. He said, "O what a capi-
> tal title!" and from that time I had settled in my mind that
> this should be my first story. (*Letters, 2, 407.*)

This account was written eighteen months after the fact, and
while there is no reason to question the accuracy of the information, it is not so suggestive of the state of George Eliot's mind
immediately preceding the composition of "Amos Barton" as the
entries which she made in her journal during the summer of 1856.
The Leweses had been at Ilfracombe during most of May and
June collecting data for his *Sea-Side Studies.* In July, George Eliot
entered in her journal a piece called "Recollections of Ilfracombe,"
toward the close of which she writes:

> I never before longed so much to know the names of things
> as during this visit to Ilfracombe. The desire is part of the
> tendency that is now constantly growing in me to escape from

2. June 26–August 9, 1856.

2

all vagueness and inaccuracy into the daylight of distinct, vivid ideas. The mere fact of naming an object tends to give definiteness to our conception of it—we have then a sign that at once calls up in our minds the distinctive qualities which mark out for us that particular object from all others. (*Letters*, 2, 251.)

The tendency of mind indicated here was, of course, highly conducive to the writing of fiction, and one sees plainly foreshadowed the careful descriptive accuracy of the stories George Eliot was shortly to publish. On July 20, she notes:

The fortnight has slipped away without my being able to show much result from it. I have written a review of the "Lover's Seat" for the *Leader*, and jotted down some recollections of Ilfracombe; besides these trifles and the introduction to an article already written, I have done no *visible* work. But I have absorbed many ideas and much bodily strength; indeed, I do not remember ever feeling so strong in mind and body as I feel at this moment. . . . I am anxious to begin my fiction writing.[3]

There is no way of knowing whether it was before or after the writing of this last entry that the "dreamy" conception of "Amos Barton" took place. It is clear, however, that what seemed to be a sudden inspiration was in fact the result of this period of inward marshaling of strength and powers, that the need for expression grew directly out of the desire to "escape from all vagueness and inaccuracy."

On August 9, the Leweses returned to their lodgings in Richmond. George Eliot's next reference to her plans for writing fiction is the journal entry for August 18: "Walked in Kew Park

3. Autograph Journal, 1854–1861, Beinecke Rare Book and Manuscript Library, Yale; hereafter designated Autograph Journal.

and talked with G. of my novel."[4] She was prevented from actually beginning work on the story, however, by commitments to the *Westminster Review,* but by September 19 she had written the promised articles,[5] and on the 23rd she notes in her journal: "Began to write 'The Sad Fortunes of the Reverend Amos Barton,' which I hope to make one of a series called 'Scenes of Clerical Life.'"

"Amos Barton" was completed on November 5, and the next day Lewes sent the manuscript to John Blackwood, the editor of *Blackwood's Edinburgh Magazine,* as having been "submitted to me by a friend who desired my good offices with you." *(Letters, 2,* 269.) Lewes wrote that the story was to be one of a series consisting of "tales and sketches illustrative of the actual life of our country clergy about a quarter century ago; but solely in its *human* and *not at all* in its *theological* aspect," that the stories would be free from doctrinal or polemical intent, and that the author had "begged me particularly to add that . . . the tone throughout will be sympathetic and not at all antagonistic." *(Letters, 2, 269.)*

In his reply, Blackwood wrote that he found the story "unquestionably very pleasant reading," praised its humor, pathos, and "happy turn of expression," and congratulated the author "on being worthy of the honours of print and pay." *(Letters, 2, 272.)* He expressed reluctance, however, to commit himself to publication of the series until he had seen more of it. He also made several mild criticisms of the story, one of which is of particular interest as foreshadowing so much later comment on George Eliot's work. "Perhaps," he wrote, "the author falls into the error of trying too much to explain the characters of his actors by descriptions instead of allowing them to evolve in the action of the story." When Lewes wrote that his "clerical friend" was somewhat discouraged by the letter, the publisher replied at once that he had "so high an opinion of this first *Tale*" that he was quite willing to set aside

4. Ibid.
5. Ibid., entries for September 12 and September 19, 1856.

his usual editorial caution and begin publication in *Blackwood's* as soon as possible. (*Letters, 2, 273; 2, 275*.) Lewes' answer to this gives evidence of both the diffidence and the ambitiousness with which George Eliot assumed the role of novelist:

> Your letter has greatly restored the shaken confidence of my friend, who is unusually sensitive, and unlike most writers is more anxious about *excellence* than about appearing in print—as his waiting so long before taking the venture proves. He is consequently afraid of failure though not of obscurity; and by failure he would understand that which I suspect most writers would be apt to consider as success— so high is his ambition. (*Letters, 2, 276*.)

As proposed, the first installment of "Amos Barton" appeared in *Blackwood's* in January 1857, and called forth the first public notice of George Eliot's fiction, a brief reference in the *Critic's* monthly survey of current magazines:

> *Blackwood* opens the year attractively with the first of a promised series of tales, illustrative of Clerical Life, and this one is so truthful in its portraiture, that it is manifestly drawn from life. . . . There is just the slightest dash of humour which gives piquancy to the sketches.[6]

"Amos Barton" was concluded in the February number. The second "scene," "Mr. Gilfil's Love Story," followed immediately, in four installments beginning in March. "Janet's Repentance" appeared in five installments, beginning in July.[7] George Eliot had planned at first to continue the series beyond "Janet's Repentance"; in "How I Came to Write Fiction" she writes that she especially "longed to tell the story of the Clerical Tutor" but abandoned the idea because of "annoyance at Blackwood's want

6. *The Critic* (January 15, 1857), p. 39.
7. "Amos Barton" is approximately 30,000 words long, "Mr. Gilfil's Love Story" 45,000, and "Janet's Repentance" 60,000.

of sympathy in the first two parts of 'Janet.' "[8] She at one time thought also of writing a "scene" based on the incident in the career of her Methodist aunt, Mrs. Samuel Evans, which became the "germ" of *Adam Bede*.[9] It seems probable, however, that even had Blackwood been enthusiastic about "Janet's Repentance" George Eliot would have closed the series in favor of the greater inspiration of *Adam Bede*. While still at work on the third "scene" she wrote Blackwood: "I have a subject in mind which will not come under the limitation of the title 'Clerical Life,' and I am inclined to take a large canvas for it, and write a novel." (*Letters*, 2, 381.) That *Adam Bede* was begun less than two weeks after "Janet's Repentance" was completed[1] testifies to the strength of her inspiration for the novel, and perhaps also indicates that she considered the writing of the three short stories a sufficient trying-out of her powers as a novelist.

In his first letter to Blackwood concerning *Scenes of Clerical Life*, Lewes said that the object of the series would be to represent the clergy "like any other class with the humours, sorrows, and troubles of other men." (*Letters*, 2, 269.) It is this overall governing intention which gives the series such unity as it has, for the three heroes are very dissimilar types and their individual dramas are acted out in widely varying milieus, though the three separate worlds presented are, geographically, close together.

---

8. *Letters*, 2, 409. Blackwood's objections to the story are discussed in Chap. 2, below. Professor Haight has suggested to me that the "Clerical Tutor" might have been based on the career of John Sibree, Jr., an acquaintance of George Eliot's Coventry days. Sibree, who had become acquainted with the Higher Criticism while studying theology at Halle, gave George Eliot Greek lessons when she first went to live at Foleshill in 1841. See *Letters*, *1*, lxxiv, and Mary H. Deakin, *The Early Life of George Eliot* (Manchester, 1913), p. 52.

9. "History of 'Adam Bede,'" *Letters*, 2, 502.

1. George Eliot's journal shows that "Janet's Repentance" was finished on October 9, 1857, and *Adam Bede* begun on October 22.

The Work and Its Reception

"The Sad Fortunes of the Reverend Amos Barton" is laid in the rural parish of Shepperton around the year 1837. Amos Barton, the curate of Shepperton Church, is an altogether undistinguished man with a good and beautiful wife, Milly. Six children and an income of only eighty pounds a year make the Bartons' life a constant struggle with debt and poverty. Amos is unpopular with his parishioners, but because of their love for Milly they overlook his shortcomings, the chief of which is tactlessness. The Countess Czerlaski, the English-born widow of a gone-to-seed Polish dancing master, herself an ex-governess, has come into the neighborhood in hopes of finding a second husband with money. She cultivates the Bartons' friendship, and they accept her at face value—Amos through a foolish susceptibility to flattery and Milly through kindly generosity and innocence. The Countess lives with her half-brother, Mr. Bridmain; when they quarrel she imposes herself on the Bartons, staying on at the vicarage for months, an addition to their expenses and a drain on Milly's already overtaxed strength. Her presence in the household becomes a subject for scandal, and the tolerance of the parish toward Amos turns to calumny. The Countess eventually leaves but bad feeling remains. When Milly dies following the birth of a seventh child, however, natural instincts of kindness and sympathy for the sorrowing Amos, whose suffering is intensified by the realization that he had made but poor return to Milly's selfless love, create a new and stronger bond between the people of the parish and their pastor. But this is not a lasting comfort, for the curacy of Shepperton is withdrawn from Amos and he is forced to move to a distant parish. In a brief epilogue he is seen returning years later to visit Milly's grave.

The romantic tone and aristocratic setting of "Mr. Gilfil's Love Story" contrast sharply with the homely simplicity of "Amos Barton." The principal action of the second "scene" takes place at Cheverel Manor, the home of Sir Christopher Cheverel, in the late eighteenth century. Sir Christopher's household includes his

7

handsome young ward, the Reverend Maynard Gilfil, who has just entered the Church, and Lady Cheverel's protegée, Caterina Sarti, a young Italian girl with a beautiful voice. Gilfil loves Caterina, but she is in love with Sir Christopher's nephew and heir, Anthony Wybrow, who has amused himself by flirting with her. When Wybrow, following Sir Christopher's wishes, proposes marriage to another girl and is accepted, Caterina is tormented by jealousy. The fiancée, Miss Assher, comes to visit at Cheverel Manor and begins to suspect some relation between Wybrow and Caterina. Wybrow leads her to believe that Caterina has thrust her love upon him, and when Miss Assher reproaches her for this, Caterina is frantic with anger and humiliation. Thinking to kill Anthony, Caterina goes to keep a rendezvous with him armed with a dagger. When she reaches the meeting place, however, she finds him lying dead, the victim of a heart attack. In an agony of shock and remorse, Caterina runs away from Cheverel Manor. Gilfil finds her and eventually, when she has recovered from an illness brought on by her unhappy passion, they are married. They go to live at Shepperton, but Caterina dies within a year. Gilfil stays on as vicar of Shepperton for forty years, becoming eccentric and whimsical but universally loved and respected.

The scene is completely changed again in "Janet's Repentance." This story is laid in the market town of Milby, around the years 1830–32. It concerns the degradation of an essentially noble woman, Janet Dempster, who, because of her husband's brutality, has taken to drink. When turned out of her home by her husband, she struggles to give up drinking and regain her self-respect. In her wretchedness she turns for help to Mr. Tryan, an Evangelical curate, and his sympathy and understanding enable her to overcome the weakness. The private drama of Janet and Robert Dempster is interwoven with the public drama of the persecution of Mr. Tryan, who is regarded as a "canting innovator" by the supporters of orthodox churchmanship, a group which includes Mr. Dempster. After Dempster's death from delirium tremens and the effects of a driving accident, the persecution loses force, and when Mr. Tryan dies, he is regretted by all. Janet is seen at the last restored to noble womanhood, devoting her life to the service of others.

The main persons and places of the *Clerical Scenes* came directly from George Eliot's recollections of her girlhood in Warwickshire. Shepperton is Chilvers Coton, the parish in which Mary Ann Evans was born and baptized, and Milby, described in "Amos Barton" as the "nearest market-town," is Nuneaton, where she was at boarding school from 1828 to 1832. Cheverel Manor is a faithful reproduction of Arbury Hall, the estate of the Newdigate family, the employers of George Eliot's father. The resemblances between characters in the stories and actual people were seen at once by Warwickshire readers, and lists were drawn up identifying almost all of the personae with real men and women, many of them still alive in 1857, who had lived in and around Nuneaton during the time in which the events described took place.[2]

Amos Barton was recognized immediately as a portrait of the Reverend John Gwyther, who had been curate of Chilvers Coton in the 1830s. *Blackwood's* London manager, Joseph Munt Langford, wrote to John Blackwood in February 1857, while "Amos Barton" was running in the magazine:

> I heard a curious thing about Amos Barton, namely that it is the actual life of a clergyman named Gwythir [sic] who at the time the incidents occurred lived at a place called, I think, Coton in one of the midland counties and who is now vicar of a small parish in Yorkshire. Indeed his daughter wrote to a lady, a friend of mine, telling her to be sure to read the story as it was their family history. (*Letters, 2, 298.*)

2. One such list is published in Charles S. Olcott, *George Eliot, Scenes and People in Her Novels* (New York, 1910), pp. 14 ff. The various characters of the stories are identified on the basis of these lists in I. G. Mudge and M. E. Sears, *A George Eliot Dictionary* (London, 1924).

9

Gwyther himself had recognized the portrait. In June 1859 he wrote to the editors of *Blackwood's:*

> I have been a subscriber to your Magazine for about 12 years, and was much perplexed when I read the 1st number of "Amos Barton"—on showing it to my Eldest Daughter she said "Who in the world could have written this—have you Papa?".... All confirmed that I was the party delineated, and that it must have been written by some one intimate with me. (*Letters, 3,* 83–84.)

"Time passed away and my pained feelings at the making public my private history abated," Gwyther continues, and after stating his suspicions concerning the author, whom he took to be a Mr. King, concludes:

> If it was he, and you have any communication with him, you may make my kind remembrances to him, and say that now the pain I felt at the first publication is past off—although I thought it unkind and taking a great liberty with a living Character—yet I fully forgive for old acquaintance sake. For we are as assured that I am intended by Amos Barton as I am of the Truth of any Fact soever. (*Letters, 3,* 84.)

The Blackwoods felt that this letter deserved acknowledgment, and George Eliot wrote the following statement, of which a copy made by John Blackwood was sent to Gwyther:

> The author of the "Scenes of Clerical Life" and "Adam Bede" begs me to inform you that he is not the Rev. W. H. King, but a much younger person, who wrote "Amos Barton" under the impression that the clergyman whose long past trial suggested the groundwork of the story was no longer living, and that the incidents, not only through the license and necessities of artistic writing, but in consequence of the writer's imperfect knowledge, must have been so varied

from the actual facts, that any one who discerned the core of truth must also recognize the large amount of arbitrary, imaginative addition.

But for any annoyance, even though it may have been brief and not well-founded, which the appearance of the story may have caused Mr. Gwyther, the writer is sincerely sorry. (*Letters, 3,* 85–86.)

While it is not likely that anyone today can separate the "core of truth" from the "arbitrary, imaginative addition," it is beyond doubt that the characters of Amos and Milly Barton are based on those of John Gwyther and his wife Emma, who died at Chilvers Coton in 1836, leaving a family of seven children. In September 1859, when the question of portraits in *Adam Bede* was a subject for speculation, George Eliot wrote to her friend Charles Bray: "There are *two* portraits in Clerical Scenes: they are, first, *Amos Barton* who however is made a much better man than he really was, and far more unimpeachable in conduct."[3] Concerning the actual incidents which make up the story, however, there is no information. In his letter to *Blackwood's,* Gwyther refers to "the Countess," but he makes no comment on her life at Chilvers Coton, and he indicates a relationship between her and the man commonly supposed to be represented by Mr. Bridmain different from that of Bridmain and the Countess Czerlaski. (*Letters, 3,* 84.) Whatever the facts of the episode which suggested the groundwork of "Amos Barton," they are essentially irrelevant to an analysis of George Eliot's art for, as she herself declared, she had no full knowledge in the matter: "The affair of the 'Countess' was never fully known to me: so far as it *was* known, it is varied from my knowledge of the alleged fact." (*Letters, 3,* 156.)

Fact can be more clearly distinguished from fiction in the case of "Mr. Gilfil's Love Story," for the Newdigate family history,

---

3. *Letters, 3,* 156. The second portrait was Lawyer Dempster in "Janet's Repentance," discussed below.

which provides the background of the story, is well documented.[4] The original of Sir Christopher Cheverel was Sir Roger Newdigate, fifth baronet, who in the late eighteenth century devoted himself to the Gothicizing of Arbury Hall, which receives detailed attention in George Eliot's story. The prototype of Caterina Sarti was a collier's daughter named Sally Shilton, who was brought up and educated by Sir Roger's wife. She married the Reverend Bernard Gilpin Ebdell, vicar of Chilvers Coton from 1786 to 1828, a tenure corresponding to Mr. Gilfil's forty years at Shepperton.[5] Unlike George Eliot's heroine, Mrs. Ebdell lived to enjoy twenty years of married life. The plot of "Mr. Gilfil's Love Story," in fact, seems to be altogether invented. As regards position and appearance, Anthony Wybrow has an original in Sir Roger Newdigate's heir, Charles Parker, but Parker's marriage to a Miss Anstruther ("Miss Assher") took place when Sally Shilton was only eleven years old. George Eliot's own comment on the writing of the story makes clear the extent of its basis in fact. In May 1858, Blackwood wrote the Leweses of a conversation he had had with Charles Newdigate Newdegate, the head of the family at that time, in which Mr. Newdegate praised the stories, said they were "all about my place and County," and offered to provide a "key to the whole characters." (*Letters*, 2, 457–58.) To this George Eliot replied:

> You were right in believing that I should like to hear Mr. Newdegate's opinion of the Stories. His testimony to the spirit in which they are written is really valuable, for I know he deserves the character you give him.
> As to details, he seems, from what you say, as likely to be

4. The fullest account of the Newdigate family in the period of "Mr. Gilfil's Love Story" is Lady Newdigate-Newdegate, *The Cheverels of Cheverel Manor,* London, 1898, a book based upon the letters and diaries of Sir Roger Newdigate's second wife, Hester, the Lady Cheverel of George Eliot's story.
5. Ebdell signed the certificate of baptism of Mary Ann Evans in 1819.

mistaken about them as he is about the authorship;[6] but it is invariably the case that when people discover certain points of coincidence in a fiction with facts that happen to have come to their knowledge, they believe themselves able to furnish a key to the whole. That is amusing enough to the author, who knows from what widely sundered portions of experience—from what a combination of subtle shadowy suggestions with certain actual objects and events, his story has been formed. Certain vague traditions about Sir Roger Newdegate (him of "Newdegate-Prize" celebrity) which I heard when I was a child are woven into the character of Sir Christopher Cheverel, and the house he improved into a charming Gothic place with beautiful ceilings, I know from actual vision—but the rest of "Mr. Gilfil's Love Story" is spun out of the subtlest web of minute observation and inward experience, from my first childish recollections up to recent years. So it is with all the other stories. It would be a very difficult thing for me to furnish a key to them myself. But where there is no exact memory of the past any story with a few remembered points of character or of incident may pass for a history. (*Letters, 2, 459–60.*)

"Janet's Repentance," like "Amos Barton," comes more directly from George Eliot's personal knowledge of actual events than "Mr. Gilfil's Love Story." She wrote Blackwood that "the story so far as regards the *persecution,* is a real bit in the religious history of England that happened about eight-and-twenty years ago." (*Letters, 2, 347.*) In the same letter, she confirms the fact that the Dempsters are based on actual people: "The real town was more vicious than my Milby; the real Dempster was far more disgusting than mine; the real Janet alas! had a far sadder end than mine."

6. Newdegate attributed the *Scenes* to Joseph Liggins, a native of Nuneaton. Liggins was later widely credited with *Adam Bede* as well, and his refusal to deny the authorship was a contributing factor in George Eliot's decision to reveal her identity.

Contemporary keys to the *Clerical Scenes* all agree in naming James Williams Buchanan, a lawyer in Nuneaton, and his wife Nancy as the originals of the Dempsters. The actual persecution of an Evangelical preacher in Nuneaton involved a clergyman named John Edmund Jones who, like Mr. Tryan, had a long last illness, and who died in 1831 at the age of thirty-four.[7] George Eliot seems not to have based her character on Mr. Jones' personality, however. When "Janet's Repentance" appeared in *Blackwood's,* his brother, William Pitman Jones, wrote to the editors to say that the story dealt with his brother's experience and that he was "utterly at a loss to conceive who could have written the statements or revived what should have been buried in oblivion." (*Letters, 2,* 375.) George Eliot rejected the identification unequivocally: "Mr. Tryan is not a portrait of any clergyman, living or dead. He is an ideal character, but I hope probable enough to resemble more than one evangelical clergyman of his day." (*Letters, 2,* 375.) The story of Janet's degradation and repentance seems also to have been "ideal." The Buchanans were never separated, and Mrs. Buchanan died some six years before her husband.[8]

In the same letter in which she acknowledged the portrait in "Amos Barton," George Eliot wrote: "No one who is not an artist knows how experience is wrought up in writing any form of poetry." (*Letters, 3,* 156.) The reference to poetry, with the implication that prose fiction is a form of poetry, is significant. In much the same way that a poem is a re-creation of experience

7. See *Letters, 2,* 375n. At the time of Jones' death, the writer of an unpublished diary now in the Nuneaton Public Library noted that Mr. Jones "was of the Evangelical School in Religion and had caused more division and quarrels on a religious score in the Town among the Church people and Dissenters than had taken place during the last ½ Century." I am indebted to Professor Haight for lending me a transcript of this diary. The identity of the writer is unknown. The statement quoted appears under the heading "Dec'r 1831."

8. *Letters, 1,* 58n.

rather than a description of it, "Amos Barton" and the other *Scenes* are re-creations. The artist, whether poet or novelist, gives form and meaning to the random matter of actuality; life may supply data for a characterization, but art must give it substantial reality. In her reply to Gwyther, George Eliot wrote of the "license and necessities of artistic writing." The artist's license in his treatment of experience is restricted only by considerations of good taste and honesty, and by the disposition of his own conscience. On this question, and in connection with *Scenes of Clerical Life*, George Eliot wrote:

> I should consider it a fault which would cause me lasting regret, if I had used reality in any other than the legitimate way common to all artists who draw their materials from their observation and experience. It would be a melancholy result of my fictions if I gave *just* cause of annoyance to any good and sensible person. But I suppose there is no perfect safeguard against erroneous impressions or a mistaken susceptibility. We are all apt to forget how little there is about us that is unique, and how very strongly we resemble many other insignificant people who have lived before us. (*Letters*, 2, 376.)

A consideration of the use of originals in *Scenes of Clerical Life* reveals both the strength and the weakness of the beginning novelist. One may count as weakness the melodramatic or pathetic turn which George Eliot gives to these stories when confronted with the necessity of inventing a plot. "Amos Barton" is probably the best of the three "scenes" because it is truest to life, full of homely realistic detail and free alike from startling incident and strong passions. "Mr. Gilfil's Love Story" begins well with a realistic picture of Mr. Gilfil's old age (a picture of Coton parish as George Eliot had actually known it), but the author's untried powers of invention fail when called upon to devise a romantic tragedy among ladies and gentlemen she had never known. Again,

Janet Dempster's drunkenness is never very believable and the romantic interest which develops between her and Mr. Tryan is obviously contrived. All this suggests a dependence upon reality natural enough in a novelist's first work. George Eliot's strength lies in the imaginative insight she brings to bear on the material of reality when she stays within the limits of her own experience. The commonplace villagers of Shepperton, an eccentric old clergyman, the domestic sorrows of a stupid man and his gentle wife, the religious ferment of a dreary provincial mill town—such materials, dull and insignificant on the surface but obviously drawn from life, George Eliot invests with an interest and appeal which struck the first readers of the *Scenes* as something quite new in English fiction.

While the popular success of *Scenes of Clerical Life* was only moderate,[9] the book made a deep and immediate impression in literary circles. Dickens and Thackeray spoke highly of it, and the critics were unanimous in their praise. Comment from all quarters bore out Blackwood's early remark that he had "lighted upon" a new author who was "uncommonly like a first class passenger." (*Letters, 2, 291.*) We know, of course, that he was right in this judgment, but however much we may admire the *Scenes* today, we cannot fully appreciate the contemporary enthusiasm for them unless we recall the literary background against which they first appeared.

In July 1858, the author of an article on Trollope in the *National Review* declared:

> The present age is the age of novels. There is no department of literature which has by the existing generation of writers

---

9. The first edition of 1050 copies was printed in January 1858; a second edition was not called for until August 1859, when 1500 copies were printed. George Eliot received £443 for the serial rights and the first edition, and an additional £200 for the second edition. See Appendix I, *Letters, 7, 359–60,* and *Letters, 2, 393.*

been more successfully cultivated, none which has been more in favour with the existing generation of readers, than that of prose fiction. . . . The press teems with novels, tales, romances innumerable, of every conceivable shade of character, quality, and substance. All the wit, fancy, and imagination of the age seems to be forced into this form of expression.[1]

In the teeming novelistic activity described here, quantity far outweighed quality. A large part of the output consisted of fashionable romances, sensational novels of the type that were to become so popular in the sixties, highly moral "uplift" novels, and stories of social or religious purpose that were merely thinly disguised tracts. The unknown writer calling herself "George Eliot" displayed qualities which placed her work clearly ahead of that of most other mid-century novelists. Aside from *Little Dorrit* and *The Virginians*—the productions of the acknowledged "greats"— only *Barchester Towers*, of all the books written and published in 1857 and 1858, could claim superiority over the *Clerical Scenes*.

The distinction of George Eliot's first fiction may be seen most clearly in relation to the work of novelists who, after Dickens and Thackeray, were considered the best in the field. Among the works in this category published in the same year as the *Scenes* were Bulwer-Lytton's artificial and facile *What Will He Do With It?* and Charles Kingsley's didactic *Two Years Ago*, a hodge-podge of sanitary reform, jingoism, and anti-slavery sentiment; the sentimental novels—*Dynevor Terrace* and *John Halifax, Gentleman* —of Charlotte Mary Yonge and Dinah Mulock; Wilkie Collins' thriller, *The Dead Secret;* and Charles Reade's *White Lies*, which George Eliot called the work of a man "gone mad with restless vanity and unveracity." (*Letters*, 2, 422.) Though their titles are still recorded in histories of literature, these books are probably as little read today as *The Morals of Mayfair, Guy Livingston*, and other popular ephemera of the mid-fifties. Slightly earlier in the

---

1. *National Review*, 7 (July 1858), 416.

decade were Kingsley's historical romances, *Hypatia* (1853) and *Westward Ho!* (1855), Reade's propagandistic *It Is Never Too Late to Mend* (1856), and Miss Yonge's most popular (and most sentimental and moralistic) tale, *The Heir of Redclyffe* (1853). In this company, *Scenes of Clerical Life* could not go unnoticed. Here was a book which, as the examination of contemporary comment will show, seemed to its first readers refreshingly free from the didacticism, the sentimentality, and the romanticism which characterized most mid-Victorian fiction.

Mrs. Gaskell, it must be noted, was also writing in the fifties, and certainly her work is superior to the books mentioned above. *Ruth* (1853) and *North and South* (1855), however, are distinctly novels of purpose, and while they have real merit simply as stories, they are limited by their didacticism in a way that the *Scenes* are not. The case of *Cranford* (1853) is rather different. The *Scenes* stand apart from this novel, as from the work of Trollope, by virtue of the moral insight which George Eliot brings to bear on her material. In *Cranford, The Warden* (1855), and *Barchester Towers* (1857), no effort is made to invest the action with any significance beyond that of the immediate and local interest of the stories themselves. Their authors claimed no moral depth for these books, and contemporary readers found none there. In the case of such delightful books as these, one would hesitate to say that the *Scenes* are better. They are, however, different, and it was with the "difference" of *Scenes of Clerical Life* that the readers of 1858 were struck.

An article in the *Saturday Review* called "A New Novelist" shows how George Eliot's contemporaries recognized at once the originality of the *Clerical Scenes*.[2] The first sentence anticipates the tenor of the whole:

> The readers of *Blackwood's Magazine* during the past year were set speculating as to the authorship of the *Scenes of*

2. *Saturday Review* (May 29, 1858), pp. 566–67.

Clerical Life, which were obviously the production of a peculiar and remarkable writer, whose style showed little or no family resemblances with that of any living author.

Declaring himself indifferent to the author's identity, the writer continues:

> It is enough for us that George Eliot is a new novelist, who to rare culture adds rare faculty, who can paint homely every-day life and ordinary characters with great humour and pathos, and is content to rely on the truth of his pictures for effect. Considering how unfamiliar most of us are with life in its romantic and adventurous forms, and with men and women of colossal proportions, it is strange that writers rarely have the courage or the talent to depict the characters and experiences which they and we know so well, but fly off at a tangent of improbability as soon as their pens touch paper. George Eliot has the courage and the talent to paint what he knows and only what he knows.

The reviewer praises the "quiet truth" of George Eliot's presentation, which, he says, "we find in few of his contemporaries," and enlarges on the theme in connection with the choice of main characters. Having described Amos Barton, he comments:

> To make a hero out of such a curate required steadfast faith in the power of truth, and disregard of conventions. The same disregard of circulating-library principles is seen in the portrait of the Rev. Mr. Gilfil. . . . We are introduced to Mr. Gilfil when he is old; his romance has been lived; he has loved and suffered; but instead of our being called upon to weep over a wasted life, and to pity a noble ruin, we are forced to love and admire a quite ordinary mortal.

The reviewer also admires George Eliot's "boldness" in dealing with a woman's drunkenness in "Janet's Repentance," and praises the unliterary quality of the whole series:

> The characters are not only true portraits, but they are living beings. Their feelings and motives are seen to be part and parcel of their natures and conditions, their talk is individual, belongs strictly to *them,* and not to the author. Hence even the little scraps of village gossip, or kitchen talk, introduced to carry on the story, have an independent life-like value. Whether the dialect is correctly or incorrectly given, we cannot say, but we are quite certain that the language is that of peasants, farmers, and servants, not the language of fiction.

The discussion concludes with the comment that George Eliot is either "a new writer—or, if a writer already known, one who has adopted a decidedly new style."

The critic for the *Times,* Samuel Lucas, also notes with approval George Eliot's devotion to the truth of everyday life and the absence of romantic exaggeration in the *Scenes.*[3] Observing that "the sources of interest are chiefly domestic and homely, and that there is a careful study of familiar types, and an absence of exaggeration in their treatment," Lucas particularly praises the originality of George Eliot's picture of Mr. Gilfil: "Here the author rejects the conventional usage of representing a bereaved hero as unhappy ever after." Unlike "the ordinary heroes of romance in similar circumstances," Mr. Gilfil "takes an interest not only in the duties but in the pleasures of life which still remain to him." Lucas notes further that the charm of the story

> is sustained by an adherence to probability and by the allowance for influences which the incidents alone do not involve, but which we know to make up a large proportion of every man's life. The artificial elements of the story are thus kept

3. *The London Times* (January 2, 1858), p. 9.

within bounds, the tendency to sacrifice to their exigencies is compensated by a reference to the actual results of experience, and a closer resemblance than is usual is thus established between the conceptions of fiction and the realities of the world.

To the series as a whole he attributes "a sobriety which is shown to be compatible with strength, clear and simple descriptions, and a combination of humour and pathos in depicting ordinary situations." The review closes with the statement that "a writer who can work out his simple theme thus quietly and effectively needs no further commendation or exhibition on our part."

The highest praise came from the weekly, *John Bull.* The following sentence will suffice to indicate the tone of the review:

> Mr. Eliot will not avail himself of the slow approaches by which other writers timidly seek to beguile, surprise, or circumvent their readers into sympathy for the joys and sorrows of their heroes and heroines: strong in his knowledge of the human heart, he marches like a conqueror into that citadel, which surrenders to him at once.[4]

As a book which had already appeared in serial form and as the first production of an unknown author, *Scenes of Clerical Life* was not widely reviewed. In addition to the three reviews quoted above, there were notices in the *Globe* and the *Statesman,*[5] a review in the *Literary Gazette,* and articles touching tangentially on the book in the *Revue des deux mondes* and the *National Review.*[6]

---

4. *John Bull's Weekly* (February 8, 1858), p. 91.

5. In her journal (January 23, 1858), George Eliot notes: "There appeared a well-written and enthusiastic article on the book in *'The Statesman.'* We hear there was a poor article in the *Globe*—a feebly [?] written praise—the previous week, but beyond this we have not yet heard of any notices from the Press." I have been unable to find copies of these newspapers.

6. *Literary Gazette* (January 23, 1858), pp. 82–83; *Revue des deux mondes* (May 15, 1858), pp. 305–31; *National Review,* 7 (October 1858), 487–515.

The last two are essentially essays on English religious life, and contain little of critical significance.[7]

Neither the Leweses nor John Blackwood could have been surprised at the favorable reception given the *Scenes*, for it only confirmed the private comments which had reached them during the serial run of the stories. George Eliot was most pleased by that of Albert Smith, who wrote Blackwood from London:

> Nothing has delighted me so much for a long time as that story of "Amos Barton" in the Magazine. . . . You will be pleased to hear there is but one opinion about its excellence. Thack.'s eyes sparkled through his spectacles as he spoke of it yesterday. (*Letters*, 2, 293n.; 2, 298.)

In April, Blackwood wrote the Leweses that "Thackeray spoke to me a good deal about the series and thinks highly of it" (*Letters*, 2, 322), and in June (from London): "I hear nothing but applause of the power of Gilfil." (*Letters*, 2, 345.) The Reverend G. C. Swayne, a regular contributor to *Blackwood's* and Senior Dean of Corpus Christi College, Oxford, probably expressed the thought of many early readers when he wrote: "I forgot to speak of Amos Barton in my last to you, what a charming tale it is!—and yet without any straining for effect or incident; it reminds me in its tender simplicity of the Vicar of Wakefield more than anything I have read in a long time."[8]

---

7. The French critic devotes himself to the thesis that George Eliot favors a celibate clergy, a fact which he deduces from the circumstance that Mr. Tryan, a bachelor, is the only really effective clergyman in the *Scenes*. In the *Literary Gazette* review, George Eliot is linked with Boccaccio as one who "feels that 'the clerical sex' will afford him the fairest field" for the display of "quaint humour."

8. *Letters*, 2, 300. George Eliot found the comparison gratifying: "Dear old 'Goldie' is one of my earliest and warmest admirations and I don't desire a better fate than to lie side by side with him in people's memories." (*Letters*, 2, 303.)

In his first letter to George Eliot, Blackwood had indicated the prospect of republishing the series as a separate book, and preparations for this were begun as soon as "Janet's Repentance" was completed. *Scenes of Clerical Life,* in two volumes, appeared in January 1858, and George Eliot had copies sent, as from the publisher, to Dickens, Thackeray, Tennyson, Ruskin, Froude, Mrs. Carlyle, Michael Faraday, and Arthur Helps, one of Lewes' best friends. Dickens, Mrs. Carlyle, Froude, and Faraday wrote to George Eliot in return, and their letters offer an interesting sidelight on her entrance into the literary world.

Faraday's is a routine expression of thanks for "a very pleasant relief from mental occupation among my own pursuits." Froude was less formal and more specific. "I do not know when I have experienced a more pleasant surprise," he wrote, "than when on opening a book parcel two mornings ago, I found it to contain *'Scenes of Clerical Life'* 'from the author.' "[9] George Eliot was particularly pleased that he should single out "Janet's Repentance" for special notice. Froude's comment is akin to that of the reviewers who noted the unconventionality of the new author: "I do not often see *Blackwood,* but in accidental glances I had made acquaintance with 'Janet's Repentance,' and had found there something extremely different from general Magazine Stories."

Mrs. Carlyle was effusive. She read the book, she wrote,

during one of the most (physically) wretched nights of my life; sitting up in bed, unable to get a wink of sleep for fever and sore throat; and it helped me through that dreary night, as well—better than the most sympathetic helpful friend watching by my bedside could have done! (*Letters,* 2, 425–26.)

---

9. For a copy of Froude's letter see George Eliot's journal entry for January 21, 1858; for Faraday's see J. W. Cross, *George Eliot's Life as Related in Her Letters and Journals* (3 vols. Edinburgh and London, 1885), 2, 12.

Chapter One

The implied comparison which Mrs. Carlyle makes between the *Scenes* and the ordinary run of mid-Victorian novels is interesting:

> You will believe that the book needed to be something more than a "new novel" for me; that I *could* at my years, and after so much reading, read it in positive torment, and be beguiled by it of the torment! that it needed to be the one sort of Book, however named, that still takes hold of me, and that grows rarer every year—a *human* book—written out of the heart of a live man, not merely out of the brain of an author—full of tenderness and pathos without a scrap of sentimentality, of sense without dogmatism, of earnestness without twaddle—a book that makes one *feel friends,* at once and for always, with the man or woman who wrote it!

The highest praise of all came from Dickens. His enthusiasm, even after one makes allowance for his being an editor on the lookout for new talent, is impressive.

> I have been so strongly affected by the two first tales in the book you have had the kindness to send me through Messrs. Blackwood, that I hope you will excuse my writing to you to express my admiration of their extraordinary merit. The exquisite truth and delicacy, both of the humor and the pathos of those stories, I have never seen the like of; and they have impressed me in a manner that I should find it very difficult to describe to you, if I had the impertinence to try. (*Letters, 2,* 423–24.)

Dickens goes on to state his certainty (of what none of the others had suspected) that "George Eliot" is a woman,[1] and concludes:

---

1. The *Scenes* are presented as the reminiscence of a native of the vicinity described, and several touches in the stories indicate that the narrator is a man. "There come moments when one almost determines never again to oppose anything but dead silence to an angry woman" ("Mr. Gilfil's Love Story," Chap. 12), seems a man's reflection; and the passage in "Janet's Repentance" beginning "Several of us had just assumed coat-tails" (Chap. 5) is of course

You will not suppose that I have any vulgar wish to fathom your secret. I mention the point as one of great interest to me—not of mere curiosity. If it should ever suit your convenience and inclination, to show me the face of the man or woman who has written so charmingly, it will be a very memorable occasion to me. If otherwise, I shall always hold that impalpable personage in loving attachment and respect, and shall yield myself up to all future utterances from the same source, with a perfect confidence in their making me wiser and better.

"There can hardly be a climax of approbation for me after this," George Eliot wrote when she forwarded this letter to John Blackwood. (*Letters, 2,* 424.)

One notes in all the early comment on the *Scenes* the emphasis on the truthfulness of the presentation and the depth of the author's insight. That a novelist could faithfully depict perfectly ordinary people and scenes and yet give them a significance which held the reader's interest and even moved him deeply was, in 1858, a new and remarkable achievement in fiction. New, too, was the experience of having one's attention directed to the conflict of moral qualities rather than to the play of passion and circumstance, to problems of humanity rather than combinations of character. The careful delineation of inner feelings and the tracing of their evolution, the absence of picturesque or romantic exaggeration, the sympathetic presentation of characters like Amos Barton, old Mr. Gilfil, and Mr. Tryan, who if admitted at all into other books would have been comic figures—these were the qualities of a "peculiar and remarkable writer."

---

unequivocal. Unlike Dickens, most contemporary readers seem to have identified author and narrator. Mrs. Carlyle, for instance, imagined "George Eliot" to be "a man of middle age, with a wife from whom he had got those beautiful feminine touches in his book, a good many children, and a dog that he has as much fondness for as I have for my little Nero!" (*Letters, 2,* 426.)

Chapter One

Fame and big sales were to come twelve months later with the publication of *Adam Bede;* for the moment, the new novelist could find satisfaction in the knowledge that thoughtful readers had recognized a strong and original talent in her work. Had her first book been misunderstood or ignored, George Eliot might very well have given up the writing of fiction, so diffident was she of her powers. Fortunately the signs of approval were not wanting. They were from sources she could respect, and were sufficiently numerous to encourage her to proceed confidently with *Adam Bede.*

2. THEORY AND PRACTICE

In *Scenes of Clerical Life* George Eliot put into practice a theory of fiction formulated during the years of editing and reviewing which immediately preceded the beginning of her career as a novelist. From September 1851 until she went to Germany with Lewes in July 1854 she was assistant editor of the *Westminster Review*.[1] The union with Lewes did not, however, mark the end of her connection with the magazine for she contributed several long articles after that time, and from July 1855 to January 1857, she wrote the section on belles-lettres which was a regular feature of the *Westminster*'s review of contemporary literature.[2] In writing about the work of others, George Eliot naturally thought long and carefully about the nature of literature and the aims and

1. For an account of the *Westminster Review* at this period and of George Eliot's association with the publisher John Chapman, see Gordon S. Haight, *George Eliot and John Chapman* (New Haven, 1940), pp. 28–85.

2. For George Eliot's principal contributions to the *Westminster Review* in 1855–56, see *George Eliot and John Chapman*, p. 36n., or *Letters*, Appendix I, 7, 358–59. During the same period George Eliot also contributed occasional reviews and articles to the *Leader* and the *Saturday Review*. For *Leader* articles, see *Letters*, General Index, 7, 472; for *Saturday Review, Letters*, 2, 227n.

methods of novelists. Thus when she came to write fiction herself, she had certain very clear ideas of what she meant to accomplish.[3]

In an article written a few weeks before she began work on "Amos Barton," George Eliot speaks of "the sacredness of the writer's art."[4] Probably no novelist ever had a greater awareness of the responsibilities connected with the writing of fiction, and few could have been more sincere in saying, as she said during the composition of *Scenes of Clerical Life,* "Writing is part of my religion."[5] A statement in one of her letters enables us to understand the way in which literature and religion were related in her thinking. "I begin to feel for other people's wants and sorrows a little more than I used to do," she wrote to Charles Bray in 1853. "Heaven help us! said the old religions—the new one, from its very lack of that faith, will teach us all the more to help one another." (*Letters, 2,* 82.) To George Eliot, there was no means so effective as literature for teaching us to feel for the wants and sorrows of others, to love one another so that we may help one another. Her most explicit statement of this belief is in an article called "The Natural History of German Life," dealing with two books by the German novelist, W. H. Riehl:

> The greatest benefit we owe to the artist, whether painter, poet, or novelist, is the extension of our sympathies. Appeals founded on generalizations and statistics require a sympathy ready-made, a moral sentiment already in activity; but a picture of human life such as a great artist can give, surprises even the trivial and the selfish into that attention to what is

3. There have been several studies in recent years of George Eliot's critical principles; for a more detailed account of her theory of fiction than is given here, see Richard Stang, "The Literary Criticism of George Eliot," *PMLA,* 72 (December 1957), 952–61; and William J. Hyde, "George Eliot and the Climate of Realism," *PMLA,* 72 (March 1957), 147–64.

4. "Silly Novels by Lady Novelists," *Westminster Review,* 66 (October 1856), 460. *Westminster Review* is hereafter designated *WR.*

5. Letter to Miss Hennell, August 19, 1857, *Letters, 2,* 377. At this time she was at work on "Janet's Repentance," Part IV.

apart from themselves, which may be called the raw material of moral sentiment. When Scott takes us into Luckie Mucklebackit's cottage, or tells the story of "The Two Drovers,"—when Wordsworth sings to us the reverie of "Poor Susan,"—when Kingsley shows us Alton Locke gazing yearningly over the gate which leads from the highway into the first wood he ever saw,—when Hornung paints a group of chimney-sweepers,—more is done towards linking the higher classes with the lower, towards obliterating the vulgarity of exclusiveness, than by hundreds of sermons and philosophical dissertations.[6]

The idea expressed here occurs throughout George Eliot's critical writings, in brief reviews as well as in long articles. Characteristic of the former is her commendation of *Rachel Gray* on the grounds that it "undertakes to impress us with the everyday sorrows of our commonplace fellow-men, and so to widen our sympathies."[7]

We may see from another of George Eliot's letters to Mr. Bray that she considered the extension of human sympathy the prime requisite for moral progress as well as the greatest benefit gained from art. "My own experience and development deepen every day my conviction that our moral progress may be measured by the degree in which we sympathize with individual suffering and individual joy," she wrote in November 1857. (*Letters*, 2, 403.) If morality is based upon sympathy and if it is through art that this sympathy is most effectively created and nourished, it follows that the mission of art is moral in character. This idea is clearly stated in George Eliot's review of Ruskin's *Modern Painters*, Volume III:

> The fundamental principles of all just thought and beautiful action or creation are the same, and in making clear to ourselves what is best and noblest in art, we are making clear

6. *WR*, 66 (July 1856), 54.
7. *Leader* (January 5, 1856), p. 19.

to ourselves what is best and noblest in morals; in learning
how to estimate the artistic products of a particular age according to the mental attitude and external life of that age,
we are widening our sympathy and deepening the basis of
our tolerance and charity.[8]

The foundation of George Eliot's artistic credo, then, is that art
serves morality by widening men's sympathies. This is the central
thought of all her criticism in the fifties and the principle behind
Scenes of Clerical Life.[9]

Related to her belief in the moral value of art, particularly to
her view of the novelist as moralist, is her strong feeling about
didacticism in literature. That the novelist may teach she has no
doubt. In a review of Charles Kingsley's *Westward Ho!* she writes:

If he would confine himself to his true sphere, he might be
a teacher in the sense in which every great artist is a teacher
—namely, by giving us his higher sensibility as a medium,
a delicate acoustic or optical instrument, bringing home to
our coarser senses what would otherwise be unperceived by
us.[1]

But Kingsley does not confine himself to his true sphere; instead
of presenting his men and women simply as he sees them and
letting the reader draw his own conclusions from their story,
Kingsley "drops into the homily as readily as if he had been 'to
the manner born,' "[2] and shows himself more preacher than
artist:

Mr. Kingsley's necessity for strong loves and strong hatreds,
and his determination to hold up certain persons as models,

8. *WR*, 65 (April 1856), 626.
9. The origins of the doctrine of sympathy and its operation in the *Scenes*
are discussed in the next chapter.
1. *WR*, 64 (July 1855), 289.
2. Ibid.

is an obstacle to his successful delineation of character, in which he might otherwise excel. As it is, we can no more believe in and love his men and women than we could believe in and love the pattern-boy at school, always cited as a rebuke to our aberrations. Amyas Leigh would be a real, loveable fellow enough if he were a little less exemplary, and if Mr. Kingsley would not make him a text to preach from, as we suppose he is accustomed to do with Joshua, Gideon, and David. Until he shakes off this parsonic habit he will not be able to create truly human characters, or to write a genuine historical romance.[3]

It is interesting to see George Eliot reject novel after novel on the grounds of didacticism, the charge most commonly leveled against her own work by unfriendly critics. It is apparent, however, that she interprets the term more narrowly than we do today. A novel was not considered didactic because it provided moral instruction; rather, the term is applied to those novels in which the author's views and his eagerness to persuade lead him to falsify his picture in order to make a particular point. In her review of a book by Hendrick Conscience, a Flemish novelist, George Eliot points out its

fatal defect of being written in the spirit of the apologue, wherein the men and women speak and act in order to prove a moral, or to rouse some sentiment in the reader, and not as a result of any natural combination of character and circumstance.[4]

Elsewhere she says that "when a novelist is quite sure that she has a theory which suffices to illustrate all the difficulties of our earthly existence, her novels are too likely to illustrate little else than

3. Ibid., pp. 209–91.
4. *WR*, 64 (October 1855), 612.

her own theory."[5] And again, speaking of "novels that flatter a prejudice, that speak the lingo of a clique, or that further the purposes of party propagandism," she says that they are "novels in which cleverness goes to work with a narrow intention, and accomplishes what it intends; they are 'Tales for the Times,' and vanish with the times."[6]

Didacticism, interpreted as narrow special pleading, is alien to everything in George Eliot's concept of art. It is most reprehensible as an indication of moral insincerity. The plainest statement of this view is found in her article on Edward Young, the last which she wrote for the *Westminster*. The first sentence in the following quotation, it will be noted, provides additional proof of the identification in George Eliot's thought of morality with sympathy:

> Another indication of Young's deficiency in moral, *i.e.*, in sympathetic emotion, is his unintermitting habit of pedagogic moralizing. . . . In proportion as morality is emotional, *i.e.*, has affinity with Art, it will exhibit itself in direct sympathetic feeling and action, and not as the recognition of a rule. Love does not say, "I ought to love"—it loves. Pity does not say, "It is right to be pitiful"—it pities. Justice does not say, "I am bound to be just"—it feels justly. It is only where moral emotion is comparatively weak that the contemplation of a rule or theory habitually mingles with its action; and in accordance with this, we think experience, both in literature and life, has shown that the minds which are pre-eminently didactic—which insist on a "lesson," and despise everything that will not convey a moral, are deficient in sympathetic emotion.[7]

5. Review of *Hertha,* by Frederika Bremer; *WR,* 66 (October 1856), 576.
6. Review of *Perversion, or the Causes and Consequences of Infidelity; WR,* 66 (July 1856), 258.
7. "Worldliness and Other-Worldliness: The Poet Young," *WR,* 67 (January 1857), 36–37.

For a contrast to Young, George Eliot turns to Cowper:

> See how a lovely, sympathetic nature manifests itself in spite
> of creed and circumstance! Where is the poem that sur-
> passes the "Task" in the genuine love it breathes . . . in truth-
> fulness of perception and sincerity of presentation—in the
> calm gladness that springs from a delight in objects for their
> own sake, without self-reference—in divine sympathy with
> the lowliest pleasures, with the most short-lived capacity for
> pain?[8]

While Cowper is not didactic, he nevertheless teaches. In describing his manner of teaching, George Eliot describes the manner
which is to be her own:

> He compels our colder natures to follow his in its manifold
> sympathies, not by exhortations, not by telling us to meditate
> at midnight, to "indulge" the thought of death, or to ask
> ourselves how we shall "weather an eternal night," *but by
> presenting to us the object of his compassion truthfully and
> lovingly.*[9]

If didacticism is first to be condemned as destructive of moral
values, it is hardly less pernicious for the false view of life to
which it gives rise. Perhaps there is no real distinction to be made
here, for in both cases the essential point is the lack of truth in
art. It is convenient, however, to distinguish between the insincerity of the artist and the falsity of his picture. George Eliot's
main objection to Kingsley's didacticism was that it prevented his
creating "truly human characters." A more extended statement of
this danger of didacticism is found in her article "Silly Novels by
Lady Novelists." Written immediately before "Amos Barton," her

8. Ibid., p. 39.
9. Ibid., p. 40.

remarks here are of particular interest for the light they cast on the book she is shortly to write:

> The most pitiable of all silly novels by lady novelists are what we may call the oracular species—novels intended to expound the writer's religious, philosophical, or moral theories. . . . You will rarely meet with a lady novelist of the oracular class who is diffident of her ability to decide on theological questions,—who has any suspicion that she is not capable of discriminating with the nicest accuracy between the good and evil in all church parties,—who does not see precisely how it is that men have gone wrong hitherto,— and pity philosophers in general that they have not had the opportunity of consulting her. Great writers, who have modestly contented themselves with putting their experience into fiction, and have thought it quite a sufficient task to exhibit men and things as they are, she sighs over as deplorably deficient in the application of their powers. "They have solved no great questions"—and she is ready to remedy their omission by setting before you a complete theory of life and manual of divinity in a love story, where ladies and gentlemen of good family go through genteel vicissitudes, to the utter confusion of Deists, Puseyites, and ultra-Protestants, and to the perfect establishment of that particular view of Christianity which either condenses itself into a sentence of small caps, or explodes into a cluster of stars on the three hundred and thirtieth page. It is true, the ladies and gentlemen will probably seem to you remarkably little like any you have had the fortune or misfortune to meet with, for, as a general rule, the ability of a lady novelist to describe actual life and her fellow-men, is in inverse proportion to her confident eloquence about God and the other world, and the means by which she usually chooses to conduct you to

true ideas of the invisible is a totally false picture of the visible.[1]

If in this article George Eliot seems to be breaking butterflies upon the rack, the justification must be her indignation at the violation of principles which she considered sacred. To falsify the facts of human experience in the interest of narrow personal opinions would be, for her, an offense of the gravest order against both art and morality. Her belief on this point is too profound to lend itself to the light satire she intended in writing of "silly novels." A better expression of her feeling is found in the article on Riehl:

> Art is the nearest thing to life; it is a mode of amplifying experience and extending our contact with our fellow-men beyond the bounds of our personal lot. All the more sacred is the task of the artist when he undertakes to paint the life of the People. Falsification here is far more pernicious than in the more artificial aspects of life. It is not so very serious that we should have false ideas about evanescent fashions— about the manners and conversations of beaux and duchesses; but it is serious that our sympathy with the perennial joys and struggles, the toil, the tragedy, and the humour in the life of our more heavily-laden fellow-men, should not be per-verted, and turned toward a false object instead of the true one.[2]

In the next paragraph of the article George Eliot suggests the moral foundation of her theory of realism—namely, that since genuine sympathy must comprehend the ugly as well as the beautiful in its object, life must be shown as it is, not as it might or should be:

1. *WR*, 66 (October 1856), 449–50.
2. *WR*, 66 (July 1856), 54.

This perversion is not the less fatal because the misrepresenta-
tion which gives rise to it has what the artist considers a
moral end. The thing for mankind to know is, not what are
the motives and influences which the moralist thinks *ought*
to act on the labourer or the artisan, but what are the motives
and influences which *do* act on him. We want to be taught
to feel, not for the heroic artisan or the sentimental peasant,
but for the peasant in all his coarse apathy, and the artisan
in all his suspicious selfishness.[3]

In this last sentence the most important aspects of George Eliot's
theory of fiction coalesce: the concept that literature should teach;
the idea that fellow-feeling, which is to say sympathy, is the lesson
to be taught; the belief that the lives of peasants and artisans may
provide material for art; and, finally, the doctrine that art achieves
its end through a realistic treatment of life.

In George Eliot's critical writing, the strongest statement of
her belief that the moral mission of art is best performed by a
realistic treatment of material is, as might be expected, in her
review of *Modern Painters*. Concerning the importance of Ruskin's
work she says:

The truth of infinite value that he teaches is *realism*—the
doctrine that all truth and beauty are to be attained by a
humble and faithful study of nature, and not by substituting
vague forms, bred by imagination on the mists of feeling,
in place of definite, substantial reality. The thorough acceptance of this doctrine would remould our life.[4]

3. Ibid., pp. 54–55.
4. *WR*, 65 (April 1856), 626. In a letter to Miss Hennell, January 17, 1858,
George Eliot again expresses her high regard for Ruskin's doctrine: "I don't
know whether you look out for Ruskin's books whenever they appear. . . . I
venerate him as one of the great Teachers of the day—his absurdities on
practical points do no harm, but the grand doctrines of truth and sincerity in
art, and the nobleness and solemnity of our human life, which he teaches with
the inspiration of a Hebrew prophet, must be stirring up young minds in a

This is one of the few places in the reviews where the word "realism" occurs. More often, George Eliot suggests the concept by reference to the truthfulness of the presentation or by saying that a faithful picture is given. Realism was important to George Eliot as a means to an end. The ideal basis of human existence can be most readily understood when it is embodied in the forms of actual life, and thus she prefers to speak of truth rather than realism, for the former includes both the actual and the ideal, while the latter is likely to suggest only an exact rendering of external reality. In Lewes' "Realism in Art: Recent German Fiction," an article which appeared in the *Westminster Review* in 1858, he says: "Realism is the basis of all Art, and its antithesis is not Idealism, but Falsism."[5] This is also George Eliot's belief. In her reviews the objection is never to idealization of material; it is always to falsification.

That realism should concern itself with more than the outward appearance of things is the thought behind the glance she casts at Dickens in the article on Riehl:

> We have one great novelist who is gifted with the utmost power of rendering the external traits of our town population; and if he could give us their psychological character— their conceptions of life, and their emotions—with the same truth as their idiom and manners, his books would be the greatest contribution Art has ever made to the awakening of social sympathies.[6]

---

promising way. . . . The two last volumes of Modern Painters contain, I think, some of the finest writing of this age. He is strongly akin to the sublimest part of Wordsworth." (*Letters*, 2, 422–23.)

5. *WR*, 70 (October 1858), 493. "Unveracity" is another name for "falsism." In the letter to Miss Hennell in which she discusses Ruskin, George Eliot asks: "How could you waste your pretty eyes in reading 'White Lies'? Surely they are too precious to be spent on the inflated plagiarisms of a man gone mad with restless vanity and unveracity." (*Letters*, 2, 422.)

6. *WR*, 66 (July 1856), 55.

This statement suggests the three aspects of realism—physical, psychological, and moral—as it figures in George Eliot's thinking, and indicates the distinction that must be drawn between realism as mere literal representation and realism as the means of teaching truth.

George Eliot's artistic credo at the beginning of her career as novelist may be stated quite simply: Art has a moral purpose; the purpose is to widen human sympathy; this purpose can be achieved only by giving a true picture of life. An examination of her correspondence with John Blackwood during the composition of *Scenes of Clerical Life* will show how rigorously she applied to her own work the standard by which she judged the work of others.

In her letters and in her journal, George Eliot comments more freely about *Scenes of Clerical Life* than about anything else she ever wrote. A consideration of this comment permits a fuller understanding of her aims and a sounder evaluation of her achievement in her first work of fiction. In the light of her critical writing, it is not surprising to find that her statements about her art are concerned mostly with realism, moral purpose, and artistic integrity. As these three subjects are inextricably bound up with each other in her thinking, George Eliot's correspondence with Blackwood during the writing of the *Scenes* may best be examined chronologically, for by doing so one sees the consistency of her attitude at every point of the composition.

In a letter to George Eliot after the first installment of "Amos Barton" appeared, Blackwood wrote: "Some of my friends praise it very much; others condemn. I was rather startled by two of my familiars—about the best men going—declaring dead against Amos." (*Letters*, 2, 290.) As Blackwood does not specify reasons for the adverse criticism, George Eliot's reply is interesting as showing her consciousness of the distinctive quality of "Amos Barton" most likely to trouble readers in 1857:

In reference to artistic presentation, much adverse opinion will of course arise from a dislike to the *order* of art rather than from a critical estimate of the execution. Any one who detests the Dutch school in general will hardly appreciate fairly the merits of a particular Dutch painting. And against this sort of condemnation, one must steel oneself as best one can. (*Letters, 2,* 291–92.)

Here, perhaps, is the germ of the often-quoted passage in *Adam Bede* in which George Eliot compares her work to that of the Dutch painters.[7] One finds in the later passage a statement of the aesthetic attitude reflected in "Amos Barton":

It is for this rare, precious quality of truthfulness that I delight in many Dutch paintings, which lofty-minded people despise. I find a source of delicious sympathy in these faithful pictures of a monotonous homely existence, which has been the fate of so many more among my fellow-mortals than a life of pomp or of absolute indigence, of tragic suffering or of world-stirring actions.

George Eliot's words about the criticism of "Amos Barton" also reveal her conception of the relative importance of an artist's material and his treatment of it. The note of disparagement toward critics who base their judgments on a dislike of the *"order* of art" rather than on an estimate of the execution, reflects her belief that in a work of art the treatment rather than the subject is of first

7. Chap. 17, "In Which the Story Pauses a Little." George Eliot had previously made the analogy between realistic fiction and Dutch painting in her review of Frederika Bremer's *Hertha.* Speaking of Miss Bremer's inability to attain first-rank despite "unusual gifts," George Eliot writes: "Nothing can be more curious than the combination in her novels of the vapourishly affected and unreal with the most solid Dutch sort of realism." (*WR,* 66 [October 1856], 576.)

importance. During the composition of *Adam Bede*, George Eliot refused to tell Blackwood the story beforehand "on the ground that I would not have it judged apart from my *treatment*, which alone determines the moral quality of art." (*Letters, 2,* 503–04.) That this was already a part of her thinking at the beginning of her career is shown by the comment on "Amos Barton."

"Amos Barton" was, of course, complete when Blackwood first saw it, so he had little opportunity to make suggestions about George Eliot's handling of her material there.[8] The case was different with the other two stories, and George Eliot's reaction to his criticisms tells much about her approach to her work. When he sent the proof of "Mr. Gilfil's Love Story," Part I, Blackwood wrote:

> On the proof I have made some marks in regard to which I shall be very glad if you agree with me. The last marks affect the plot of the story but I think my objections may be obviated without any serious alteration of the plan. It is not a pleasant picture to see a good fellow loving on when the lady's heart is *openly* devoted to a Jackanapes, and I am a little puzzled as to how you are to bring the excellent Gilfil out without making him too abjectly devoted a lover for a man of character. I think the objection would be readily met by making Caterina a little less openly devoted to Wybrow and giving a little more dignity to her character. (*Letters, 2,* 297.)

George Eliot's answer to this is an important statement of her attitude toward her writing:

> You will see that I have availed myself of your suggestions on points of language. I quite recognize the justice of your

---

8. His one specific criticism of "Amos Barton" concerned the treatment of the children at the time of Milly's death. This is discussed in Chap. 4, below.

criticism on the French phrases. They are not in keeping with my story.[9]

But I am unable to alter anything in relation to the delineation or development of character, as my stories always grow out of my psychological conception of the *dramatis personae*. For example the behaviour of Caterina in the gallery is essential to my conception of her nature and to the development of that nature in the plot. (*Letters*, 2, 298–99.)

The use of the term "psychological conception" in this statement is of great significance. It is improbable that Thackeray, Dickens, Trollope, or indeed any other English novelist of the time would have spoken of his characters in this way. No more, probably, would Scott, Jane Austen, or Fielding. Here is the aspect of George Eliot's fiction which leads critics to say that she is the first modern novelist,[1] or to speak of her in more measured terms as a "landmark in the history of the modern novel."[2] One thinks of George Eliot as modern primarily because of her interest in motivation. Unlike Dickens and Trollope, she is not content simply to report the actions of her people; she must examine their minds so that their actions will be psychologically valid. When Florence Dombey runs away from home it is not because Dickens feels that this is what a girl like Florence would necessarily do in the circumstances; it is because her running away will give a new turn to the plot and because it is a thrilling incident in itself. When Caterina runs away from Cheverel Manor the contribution to the

9. The phrases deleted were: "of his own sitting-room fire, [apparently finding a sufficient *raison d'être* in] smoking" (MS fol. 14; *Blackwood, 81,* 324); and, "the effect was assisted by [a *mouvement de terrain*, the ground gradually descending] an undulation of the ground which gradually descended." (MS fol. 34; *Blackwood, 81,* 331.)

1. As Lord David Cecil does in *Victorian Novelists, Essays in Revaluation* (Chicago, 1958), p. 262.

2. Ernest A. Baker, *The History of the English Novel* (10 vols. London, 1934–39), *8,* 221.

plot is negligible—she could as well have collapsed at home and been soothed by Gilfil in her own room—but the action is rendered necessary by the demands of her character. It is a part of George Eliot's psychological conception of Caterina that she should take upon herself the guilt of Wybrow's death and feel that she had sinned against all the people who had been good to her, and that she should attempt to atone by removing herself from their lives. In this early case as in the case of all her more memorable creations, George Eliot is concerned first of all with the underlying causes of behavior. Caterina is a forerunner, insignificant in comparison perhaps but clearly conceived, of those greater characters from Arthur Donnithorne to Gwendolen Harleth whose personalities and motives George Eliot analyzes so brilliantly. Lewes found a "subtle truth in delineation of complex motive" in "Mr. Gilfil's Love Story." (*Letters, 2,* 307.) This is the kind of comment that is often made about George Eliot's later work, and it is interesting to see that the analytical character of her genius was recognized from the start. And her letter to Blackwood shows that George Eliot herself was perfectly aware of it.

Her letter contains other significant statements. "My artistic bent," she writes, "is directed not at all to the presentation of eminently irreproachable characters, but to the presentation of mixed human beings in such a way as to call forth tolerant judgment, pity, and sympathy." (*Letters, 2,* 299.) Again and again in her reviews George Eliot had held the "pattern-boy" type of character up to ridicule, so it is not surprising that she should choose "mixed" human beings as subjects for her own work. Here again the point at issue is truth: an artist must be true to his conception of an individual character and to the facts of human experience in choosing that character in the first place. George Eliot puts the case clearly in her letter:

I cannot stir a step aside from what I *feel* to be *true* in character. If anything strikes you as untrue to human nature in my delineations, I shall be very glad if you will point it out to me, that I may reconsider the matter. But alas! inconsistencies and weaknesses are not untrue. (*Letters, 2,* 299.)

Blackwood's objection to the presentation of Caterina turns upon what is essentially a point of propriety, and it reflects his conservative, conventional temper. As a publisher he would have preferred a heroine whose conduct was beyond reproach by polite standards of proper behavior for young ladies. But as Lord David Cecil points out (and he is only amplifying George Eliot's own statements to Blackwood):

> Since George Eliot began with an idea of character or situation, her plot was intended to follow not a standardized formula but what she conceived to be the logical development of that idea; and this might entail something quite different from the accepted Victorian notion of a plot. It might entail no marriage, no happy ending, no character answering to the Victorian conception of hero or heroine.[3]

It must only, George Eliot would say, tell the truth about life. Thus, if Caterina has a weakness—and such is her ungovernable passion for a worthless man[4]—it must be shown if her story is to be told at all. One is reminded of a later instance in which George Eliot's presentation of a girl in love was questioned. Concerning Bulwer-Lytton's criticism of Maggie Tulliver's feeling for Stephen Guest,[5] George Eliot wrote:

3. *Victorian Novelists, Essays in Revaluation,* pp. 267–68.

4. The "behaviour of Caterina in the gallery" to which George Eliot alludes and which probably gave rise to most of Blackwood's criticism, occurs in Chap. 2. In this scene passion wins an easy victory over reason in Caterina's struggle with her feeling about Wybrow: "Poor Tina was the slave of his voice and touch. Grief and resentment, retrospect and foreboding, vanished —all life before and after melted away in the bliss of that moment, as Anthony pressed his lips to hers."

5. In a letter to John Blackwood, May 4, 1860, Bulwer wrote: "The *indulgence* of such a sentiment for the affianced of a friend under whose roof

If I am wrong there—if I did not really know what my heroine would feel and do under the circumstances in which I have deliberately placed her, I ought not to have written this book at all, but quite a different book, if any. If the ethics of art do not admit the truthful presentation of a character essentially noble but liable to great error—error that is anguish to its own nobleness—*then,* it seems to me, the ethics of art are too narrow, and must be widened to correspond with a widening psychology. (*Letters, 3,* 317–18.)

This statement, though more strongly worded, is substantially what she wrote to Blackwood about her conception of Caterina. In both cases, one notices, the main emphasis is on the understanding of the character's psychology and on the truthful presentation of it.

During the course of the composition of "Mr. Gilfil's Love Story," John Blackwood raised one other objection, this one also relating to Caterina. George Eliot again defended her treatment on grounds of realism. The incident which troubled Blackwood occurs in Chapter 13, where Caterina, distraught by Wybrow's treatment of her, takes a dagger from the collection of armor at Cheverel Manor and rushes to a rendezvous in the woods, intending to stab her false lover. Blackwood wrote to Lewes concerning the incident:

I have grave doubts about the dagger, beautifully as the impossibility of her using it is indicated. I daresay George Eliot will kick furiously at the base idea of altering a syllable at this point, but I am pretty sure his dear little heroine would be more sure of universal sympathy if she only dreamed or felt as if she could stab the cur to the heart and I think it

---

she was, was a treachery and a meanness according to the Ethics of Art, and nothing can afterwards lift the character into the same hold on us." (*Letters, 3,* 317n.)

would be more consistent with her character than the active step of getting hold of the lethal weapon. I may be wrong however and I daresay many will prefer the *dadger*. (*Letters*, 2, 308.)

To this George Eliot replied:

I am glad you retain a doubt in favour of the 'dadger' and wish I could convert you to entire approval, for I am much more satisfied when your feeling is thoroughly with me. But it would be the death of my story to substitute a dream for the real scene. Dreams usually play an important part in fiction, but rarely, I think, in actual life.[6]
So many of us have reason to know that criminal impulses may be felt by a nature which is nevertheless guarded by its entire constitution from the commission of crime, that I can't help hoping my Caterina will not forfeit the sympathy of all my readers. (*Letters*, 2, 309.)

It is, of course, not the particular case of Caterina that is important here. The statement is significant in that it shows George Eliot's strict regard for being true to the facts of actual life, and, in the second paragraph, her concern for psychological realism in the presentation of character.

It is in connection with "Janet's Repentance" that George Eliot comments most fully and explicitly on her work in the *Scenes*. Blackwood had several reservations about the story, and in trying to make perfectly clear to him her attitude toward the material, George Eliot again shows her concern for truth in art and affirms in the strongest terms her belief in the artist's integrity. The theme of the letters about "Janet's Repentance" is the necessity she is

6. In a later letter, Blackwood explains that by dream he meant "a passing dream or thought in the mind," rather than a dream while sleeping, but admits that he now thinks "the author was quite right in his plan." (*Letters*, 2, 334.)

under to write what she feels to be true. This note is struck in the letter she wrote when sending the manuscript of Part I:

> Lewes seems to have higher expectations from the third story than from either of the preceding; but I can form no judgment myself until I have quite finished a thing and see it aloof from my actual self. I can only go on writing what I feel, and waiting for the proof that I have been able to make others feel. (*Letters*, 2, 335–36.)

In the last sentence George Eliot seems almost to be defending her treatment in advance of the criticism she anticipated from Blackwood. She knew the publisher's taste well enough by then to realize that the extremely realistic opening of "Janet's Repentance" would seem to him rather harsh. Of the opening of "Amos Barton," which is in every way much softer than that of "Janet's Repentance," Blackwood had written that at first he was afraid "that in the amusing reminiscences of childhood in church there was a want of some softening touch." (*Letters*, 2, 272.) The only manuscript evidence of "softening" is the crossing out of the following passage:

> Oh that happy time of childish veneration! It is the fashion to regret the days of easy merriment, but we forget the early bliss of easy reverence when the world seemed to us to be peopled with the great and wise, when the old weather-prognosticating gardener was our Socrates, and our spirits quailed before the clergyman without needing to be convinced of the Apostolic Succession. Words cannot convey the awe I felt for every member of the Shepperton choir. The bassoon player was a public character whom no effort of my imagination could follow into the penetralia of private life, and when he and his compeers came round at Christmas for their yearly money and beer, I clung to my mother's apron and felt a sort of polytheistic awe, as if I had thought

that these psalmodizing tosspots might be Olympian deities in disguise. Another functionary whom I endowed with illimitable science was the schoolmaster, who stood and sat in official prominence at the front corner of the Free School gallery. Alas! if the truth must be known, he was an old soldier, of aberrant orthography and disordered liver, whose pedagogic functions brought on a premature death from *delirium tremens.* But he carried himself military-wise and looked round with an imposing air of authority; and when he cuffed reprovingly the head of some too communicative schoolboy, I dreaded the implicit censure he might be passing on my own devotional bearing.[7]

As there is no evidence that Blackwood returned the manuscript of "Amos Barton" to George Eliot before the magazine proofs were set up, she presumably deleted this passage of her own accord. Perhaps she was concerned lest it appear from these lines that she was holding religious practices up to ridicule. Also, she must have realized that the tone of the passage—satirical and humorously disillusioned—was not in keeping with the affectionate nostalgia of the other opening paragraphs. It may even be that she felt that the wistful regret for lost faith implied at the beginning of this passage was too close to her own personal feeling for public expression. To judge from her correspondence with Blackwood, however, I should say that the deletion (while not mentioned specifically) mainly reflects George Eliot's desire not to be offensive in her treatment of church matters.

But to return to "Janet's Repentance," George Eliot was not surprised when Blackwood wrote, "I should have liked a pleasanter picture." (*Letters,* 2, 344.) He was troubled particularly that Dempster should be shown as so "barefaced a brute" and that "the poor wife's sufferings should have driven her to so unsentimental

---

7. MS fols. 4–5. The canceled passage immediately precedes the paragraph beginning "As for the clergyman, Mr. Gilfil," in Chap. 1.

a resource as beer." The following passage in her reply to his letter may be taken as George Eliot's manifesto of artistic freedom:

> If I were to undertake to alter Dempster's language or character, I should be attempting to represent some vague conception of what may possibly exist in other people's minds, but has no existence in my own. Such of your marginal objections as relate to a mere detail I can meet without difficulty by alteration; but as an artist I should be utterly powerless if I departed from my own conceptions of life and character. There is nothing to be done with the story, but either to let Dempster and Janet and the rest be as I *see* them, or to renounce it as too painful. I am keenly alive, at once to the scruples and alarms an editor may feel, and to my own utter inability to write under any cramping influence, and on this double ground I should like you to consider whether it will not be better to close the series for the Magazine *now*. (*Letters*, 2, 348.)

George Eliot was genuinely diffident about her powers as a novelist, and one does not doubt the sincerity of her humility when she came to be regarded as a great ethical influence, but she was never in doubt as to the rightness of her ideas of what fiction should be and do. She could grant that her execution might be faulty, but she could not compromise on the principles behind the writing. She makes this clear in the next paragraph of her letter to Blackwood, indicating at the same time what she considered the moral function of the writer to be:

> It is possible that I may not affect other minds as I intend and wish to affect them, and you are a better judge than I can be of the degree in which I may occasionally be offensive. I should like *not* to be offensive—I should like to touch every heart among my readers with nothing but loving humour,

with tenderness, with belief in goodness. But I may have failed in this case of Janet, at least so far as to have made you feel its publication in the Magazine a disagreeable risk. If so, there will be no harm done by closing the series with No. 2, as I have suggested. (*Letters, 2, 348.*)

In his letter Blackwood had noted the "harsher Thackerayan view of human nature," adding in the next paragraph: "Thackeray is I think rather disposed to claim you as a disciple of his." (*Letters, 2, 344–45.*) Toward the end of her letter, George Eliot writes:

There are too many prolific writers who devote themselves to the production of pleasing pictures, to the exclusion of all disagreeable truths for me to desire to add one to their number. In this respect, at least, I may have some resemblance to Thackeray, though I am not conscious of being in any way a disciple of his, unless it constitutes discipleship to think him, as I suppose the majority of people with any intellect do, on the whole the most powerful of living novelists.[8]

In reading this letter to Blackwood, one is struck by the perfect assurance with which the unknown author voices her opinions and by the tenacity with which she holds to them. It is not surprising that George Eliot, after years of reviewing, should come to the writing of fiction with quite definite ideas about that art, but it is perhaps out of the ordinary to find an untried novelist expressing herself so strongly to an experienced publisher. Even without the evidence of the stories themselves, Blackwood would have known that he was dealing with an artist whose standard of integrity was of the highest order. Happily, John Blackwood was the perfect publisher for George Eliot, as she herself was the

8. When "Amos Barton" first appeared, George Eliot made a point of asking Blackwood to let her know Thackeray's opinion of the story. See *Letters, 2, 298.*

first to admit,[9] and his tact, intelligence, and understanding are nowhere better demonstrated than in his reply to her letter about "Janet's Repentance." "I do not fall in with George Eliots every day," he writes, "and the idea of stopping the Series as suggested in your last letter gave me 'quite a turn' to use one of Thackeray's favourite phrases." (*Letters*, 2, 352.) That he fully understood and appreciated George Eliot's position is shown in the next to last paragraph of his letter:

> In continuing to write for the Magazine I beg of all things that you will not consider yourself hampered in any way. Of course I will say when I think you are failing to produce the effect you intend or otherwise missing the mark, but unless you write entirely from the bent of your own genius or knowledge or observation it would not be worth my while to comment at all. (*Letters*, 2, 352–53.)

Blackwood concludes with the hope "that there are many years of happy friendly and literary intercourse before us." The fundamental condition of such a relationship was given and accepted at the start, for it was during the composition of *Scenes of Clerical Life* that George Eliot claimed and was granted absolute freedom in following her artistic conscience. George Eliot seconded Blackwood's hope for the continuance of their connection in words which, as always when she writes of the aim of literature, indicate her view of the writer as moralist:

> I heartily respond to your wish that our literary intercourse may continue—for that wish includes many good things. It means that I shall go on writing what will stir men's hearts to sympathy as well as that I shall have all the pleasures

---

9. In a letter of June 2, 1857, she tells Blackwood that he "seems to have been created in pre-established harmony with the organization of a susceptible contributor." (*Letters*, 2, 335.)

and advantages involved in the possession of a generous editor. (*Letters*, 2, 353.)

During the summer of 1857, while she was at work on "Janet's Repentance," there was only one other exchange between George Eliot and her publisher which casts light on her approach to fiction. When he returned the proof of Part II, Blackwood was troubled by the description in Chapter 5 of a confirmation:

Your Bishop is doubtless a true sketch, but I wish he had been a better sample of the cloth.[1] Some allusion to the solemn and affecting sight that a confirmation ought to be would not lessen the effect of your quaint and amusing picture of the scene at Milby thirty years ago and would destroy the chance of any accusation of irreverence or wish to make the ceremony ridiculous. (*Letters*, 2, 360.)

In her reply George Eliot points out that in "Janet's Repentance" she was not concerned with "confirmation in general, or with Bishops in general, but with a particular confirmation, and a particular Bishop." (*Letters*, 2, 362.) This observation on a particular instance leads to a generalization about the nature of art and about her function as an artist:

Art must be either real and concrete, or ideal and eclectic. Both are good and true in their way, but my stories are of the former kind. I undertake to exhibit nothing as it should be; I only try to exhibit some things as they have been or

---

1. Blackwood was disturbed throughout the *Scenes* by George Eliot's unidealized clergymen. Of "Amos Barton" he wrote: "I hate anything of a sneer at real religious feeling as cordially as I despise anything like cant, and I should think this author is of the same way of thinking although his clergymen with one exception are not very attractive specimens of the body." (*Letters*, 2, 272.) When George Eliot was well along with "Janet's Repentance" he asked: "When are you going to give us a really good active working clergyman, neither absurdly evangelical nor absurdly High Church?" (*Letters*, 2, 345.)

are, seen through such a medium as my own nature gives me.[2]

This description of her work is in line with a statement she had made ten years earlier in a letter to John Sibree, Jr.: "Artistic power seems to me to resemble dramatic power—to be an intuitive perception of the varied states of which the human mind is susceptible with ability to give them out anew in intensified expression." (*Letters, 1,* 247.) It is the moral sensibility of the artist which connects the real world with the ideal; art, therefore, is essentially subjective, and the artist's responsibility is to recast the real according to his own perceptions, so that through his vision others may be led to see the ideal basis of ordinary experience. George Eliot recognizes the artist's right to shape experience so long as he does not falsify it: "Everything," she says concerning "Janet's Repentance," "is softened from the fact, so far as art is permitted to soften and yet to remain essentially true." (*Letters, 2,* 347.) The prerogative of the artist to refashion the material of actual life entails great responsibility. George Eliot indicates her awareness of this fact in the letter in which she describes her art as real and concrete:

> The moral effect of the stories of course depends on my power of seeing truly and feeling justly; and as I am not conscious of looking at things through the medium of cynicism or irreverence, I can't help hoping that there is no tendency in what I write to produce those miserable mental states. (*Letters, 2,* 362.)

2. *Letters, 2,* 362. In *Adam Bede,* Chap. 17, George Eliot says that her strongest effort is "to give a faithful account of men and things as they have mirrored themselves in my mind." The same idea is found in the review of *Westward Ho!,* quoted above, where she speaks of "the sense in which every great artist is a teacher—namely, by giving us his higher sensibility as a medium, a delicate acoustic or optical instrument, bringing home to our coarser senses what would otherwise be unperceived by us." (*WR, 64,* 289.)

External reality, for George Eliot as for Wordsworth, is the raw material which, when shaped by the moral sensibility of the artist, becomes the embodiment of ideal values. On this point Professor Basil Willey says:

> In her positive creative achievement . . . she abundantly shows the power attributed to Wordsworth by Coleridge, that of spreading the depth, height and atmosphere of the ideal world around situations, forms and incidents "of which, for the common view, custom had bedimmed all the lustre, and dried up the sparkle and the dew-drops."[3]

As the year of *Scenes of Clerical Life* drew to a close, George Eliot, now happily absorbed in *Adam Bede,* recorded in her journal her feelings about her first work. On December 19, 1857, she writes: "Alone this evening, with very thankful solemn thoughts —feeling the great and unhoped for blessings that have been given me in life."[4] Characteristically listing Lewes' successes first among her blessings, she then notes:

> I have written the *Scenes of Clerical Life*—my first book— and though we are uncertain still whether it will be a success as a separate publication, I have had much sympathy from my readers in *Blackwood,* and feel a deep satisfaction in having done a bit of faithful work that will perhaps remain like a primrose root in the hedgerow and gladden and chasten human hearts in years to come.

Her deep satisfaction stems from the fact that, as one sees from the letters to Blackwood, she had written from her heart and her experience, being true at all times to the demands of her artistic

---

3. *Nineteenth Century Studies. Coleridge to Matthew Arnold* (New York, 1949), p. 245.
4. Autograph Journal.

conscience. The sympathy from her readers told her that the principles she had followed had been, for her, the right ones—that through her faithful picture of ordinary life she had been able to "stir men's hearts to sympathy." What there was in the stories that might remain to "gladden and chasten human hearts in years to come," an examination of the work itself will show.

3. THE DOCTRINE OF SYMPATHY

In January 1860, while preparations for the publication of *The Mill on the Floss* were going forward, George Eliot wrote to John Blackwood:

> I am very anxious that the "Scenes of Clerical Life" should have every chance of impressing the public with its existence: first, because I think it of importance to the estimate of me as a writer that "Adam Bede" should not be counted as my only book; and secondly, because there are ideas presented in these stories about which I care a good deal, and am not sure that I can ever embody again. (*Letters, 3,* 240.)

The main ideas presented in *Scenes of Clerical Life* are all related to the central concept of George Eliot's moral philosophy—that part of her thinking which may be called her doctrine of sympathy. There are other elements of her thought embodied in the stories, of course—her attitude toward the parties of the Established Church, for instance, and her general feeling about the country life she had left so far behind, and certainly she would "care a good deal" about these things. But they do not find the direct expression which the word "ideas" suggests. The doctrine of sympathy, on the other hand, is so clearly expressed in the *Scenes* that one feels justified in the assumption that this is the main idea George Eliot wished to convey in the book. This is not to say that she wrote these stories just to propagate her particular gospel. As her reviews show, no one was more scornful than she of writers who set up as novelists but were really only preachers, or of those who turned to fiction primarily as a means of communicating a special interest. But as she was a novelist by virtue of artistic impulse, and one who believed that it was the artist's duty to teach, her books inevitably embodied her moral philosophy. The most cherished of her moral ideas, and the one she most wanted to express in her work, was that the highest responsibility of men is to sympathize with their fellow beings. An examination of *Scenes of Clerical Life* as an expression of George Eliot's doctrine of sympathy, therefore, is the proper starting point in studying the first work of a novelist who put the moral value of art above all other considerations.

Before turning to the stories themselves, however, it will be well to consider the origins of George Eliot's idea of sympathy, for in so doing one may place the *Scenes* in clearer perspective in relation both to the literary tradition and to mid-nineteenth-century morality. Professor Basil Willey has said that George Eliot, more than any other novelist, epitomizes her age—"her development is a paradigm, her intellectual biography a graph, of its most decided trend," he writes.[1] The doctrine of sympathy embodied in *Scenes of Clerical Life* is a case in point. In it, elements of eighteenth-century moral sentiment, Evangelical earnestness, the Romantic imagination, and Victorian humanitarianism meet in a characteristic expression of the mid-century conscience.

The roots of the doctrine presented here lie in the eighteenth-century reaction against the self-regarding ethics of Thomas Hobbes. Shaftesbury is the most important of the early theorists

1. *Nineteenth Century Studies*, pp. 204–05.

who assumed in man the existence of an innate feeling for the common good, and who felt that man's selfish affections and his social affections are not only consistent but inseparable: "moral Rectitude, or *Virtue,* must accordingly be the Advantage, and *Vice* the Injury and Disadvantage of every Creature."[2] Such followers of Shaftesbury as Francis Hutcheson and James Arbuckle systematized his hypothesis of an instinctive moral sense. Arbuckle, in particular, stressed the importance of fellow-feeling as the basis of moral action. He is also among the first to suggest the relationship of sympathy and imagination which is so important in Romantic aesthetic theory. In an essay of 1725, he notes the "wisdom of our Creator in giving us this imagining Faculty, and such a Facility of placing ourselves in Circumstances different from those we are really in, to enforce our Duty upon us, not only by Reason, but by Passion and powerful Inclination."[3] The benevolists' moral conception of sympathy was strengthened by the findings of empirical psychology. Hume, discussing the respective merits of reason and sentiment as guides to moral action, concludes that "that which renders morality an active principle . . . depends on some internal sense or feeling, which nature has made universal in the whole species,"[4] and bases almost all moral response on sympathy, the psychology of which he discusses in Book II of the *Treatise on Human Nature.* Burke applies the doctrine of sympathy in the realm of aesthetics. Writing in 1757, he calls sympathy, imitation, and ambition the principal social passions, and says of sympathy:

> It is by the first of these passions that we enter into the concerns of others; that we are moved as they are moved, and are never suffered to be indifferent spectators of almost any thing which men can do or suffer. For sympathy must be

2. *Inquiry concerning Virtue and Merit* (1699), Book II, Part I, Sect. I.
3. *Collection of Letters and Essays on Several Subjects* (2 vols. London, 1729), *I*, 34.
4. *Inquiry concerning the Principles of Morals* (1751), Sect. I.

considered as a sort of substitution, by which we are put into the place of another man, and affected in many respects as he is affected.[5]

But sympathy, for Burke as for Shaftesbury, was still primarily a matter of the will. It remained for Adam Smith, in his *Theory of Moral Sentiments* (1759), to assert the supremacy of the imagination.

Ignoring the existence of a moral sense independent of the imagination, Smith denies at the outset the ability of sympathy to function apart from the imagination:

As we have no immediate experience of what other men feel, we can form no idea of the manner in which they are affected, but by conceiving what we ourselves should feel in the like situation. Though our brother is upon the rack, as long as we ourselves are at our ease, our senses will never inform us of what he suffers. They never did and never can carry us beyond our own person, and it is by the imagination only that we can form any conception of what are his sensations. Neither can that faculty help us to this in any other way, than by representing to us what would be our own, if we were in his case. It is the impression of our senses only, not those of his, which our imaginations copy. By the imagination we place ourselves in his situation, we conceive ourselves enduring all the same torments, we enter as it were into his body, and become in some measure the same person with him.[6]

Smith's views were especially influential among such Scottish moralists and critics as Dugald Stewart, James Beattie, and John Ogilvie,[7] but his influence was by no means confined to a local

5. *A Philosophical Inquiry into the Origin of Our Ideas of the Sublime and Beautiful* (1757), Part I, Sect. 13.

6. *The Theory of Moral Sentiments* (1759), Part I, Sect. 1, Chap. 1.

7. See W. J. Bate, *From Classic to Romantic, Premises of Taste in Eighteenth Century England* (Cambridge, Mass., 1946), pp. 134–36.

circle. The detailed analysis of sympathy in the *Theory of Moral Sentiments* is probably the clearest expression of the growing moral and aesthetic tendency of the later eighteenth century, which finds expression not only in the works of Sterne, Goldsmith, and Mackenzie,[8] but in the political philosophy of William Godwin, who, in discussing self-love and benevolence, writes:

> We are able in imagination to go out of ourselves, and become impartial spectators of the system of which we are a part. We can then make an appraisement of our intrinsic and absolute value; and detect the imposition of that self-regard which would represent our own interest as of as much value as all the world beside.[9]

Smith's theory plainly foreshadows Romantic aesthetics in a significant way. One of the basic tenets of English Romantic criticism is that the imagination is capable of identifying itself with its object, that through the sympathetic imagination the artist achieves a direct experience of his object. This conception, so clearly related to Adam Smith's pronouncements, underlies the critical opinion of Coleridge and Wordsworth and is implied in Keats' statement that he was certain of nothing but "the holiness of the Heart's affections and the truth of the Imagination." It is only through the sympathetic imagination that the artist is able, as Wordsworth says, "to bring his feelings near to those of the persons whose feelings he describes, nay for short spaces of time, perhaps, to let himself slip into an entire delusion, and even confound and identify his own feelings with theirs."[1] Smith's theory

---

8. For an analysis of the relationship between Smith's theory and Sterne's work, see Kenneth MacLean, "Sterne and Adam Smith," *Journal of the History of Ideas,* 10 (1949), pp. 399–410. R. S. Crane, "Suggestions toward a Genealogy of *The Man of Feeling," ELH, 1* (1934), pp. 205–30, contains an interesting summary of the growth of sympathetic feeling in the early eighteenth century.

9. *Inquiry concerning Political Justice* (1793), Book IV, Chap. 10.

1. Preface to *Lyrical Ballads* (1800).

that the moral life is founded not in the will but in the imagination is obviously central to the thought of Wordsworth and Shelley. It lies alike behind Shelley's statement that "the great instrument of moral good is the imagination," and Wordsworth's description in the *Prelude* of that "spiritual Love" which

> acts not nor can exist
> Without Imagination, which, in truth,
> Is but another name for absolute power
> And clearest insight, amplitude of mind,
> And Reason in her most exalted mood.
>
> (XIV, 188–92.)

Wordsworth's sonnet on the absolute importance of imagination in the moral life is so clear a statement of his belief that it is worth quoting here for the light it casts on the thinking of George Eliot, whose favorite poet he was.

> "Weak is the will of Man, his judgment blind;
> Remembrance persecutes, and Hope betrays;
> Heavy is woe;—and joy, for human-kind,
> A mournful thing, so transient is the blaze!"
> Thus might he paint our lot of mortal days
> Who wants the glorious faculty assigned
> To elevate the more-than-reasoning Mind,
> And colour life's dark cloud with orient rays.
> Imagination is that sacred power,
> Imagination lofty and refined:
> 'Tis hers to pluck the amaranthine flower
> Of Faith, and round the sufferer's temples bind
> Wreaths that endure affliction's heaviest shower,
> And do not shrink from sorrow's keenest wind.

Apart from the poets, one may find in Hazlitt detailed analyses of the imaginative foundation of morality. In his essay, "On Reason and Imagination," he states, "I would not wish a better or more philosophical standard of morality, than that we should think and feel towards others as we should, if it were our own case," and goes on to show that this standard can be achieved only through the sympathetic imagination.[2] The whole of his long early essay, "On the Principles of Human Action" (1805), is devoted to the same thesis.

The Romantic emphasis on sympathetic imagination as a primary means of aesthetic and moral insight is as strong in George Eliot as in Wordsworth. "The only effect I ardently long to produce by my writings," she says in 1859, "is that those who read them should be better able to *imagine* and to *feel* the pains and joys of those who differ from themselves in everything but the broad fact of being struggling erring human creatures." (*Letters, 3,* 111.) Her juxtaposition and underscoring of "imagine" and "feel" point clearly to the source of her doctrine of sympathy. The supreme importance of causing readers to feel for others is stressed in the same letter. "If Art does not enlarge men's sympathies," she writes, "it does nothing morally." This is the theme upon which all of George Eliot's critical comment is variation.

While George Eliot's doctrine of sympathy is ultimately derived from the current of charity and good will which began to flow in the eighteenth century and which, strengthened by Rousseau's influence, became a fundamental element in the Romantic temper, it also owes much to circumstances peculiar to the nineteenth century. It reflects, for instance, the Evangelical emphasis on self-forgetfulness and social duty, which leads at one end of the scale to the emancipation of slaves and at the other to the round of provincial good works recorded in George Eliot's early letters. Mid-Victorian ideals of sympathy and benevolence also reflect a reaction against Benthamism and the ethics of an increasingly industrial age. In his essay on Bentham, written in 1838, John Stuart Mill declared that Bentham ignored not only the conscience but

2. *Collected Works of William Hazlitt* (12 vols. London, 1903), 7, 44–55. The quotation appears on pp. 47–48.

also the "love of loving, the need of a sympathizing support, or of objects of admiration and reverence."[3] The view was reflected in novels of the thirties as well. John Sterling's Arthur Coningsby thought Benthamism degrading because it overlooked "the nobler sympathies and convictions of mankind," and F. D. Maurice's Eustace Conway goes through a Benthamite period in which only deep impulses of humanity save him from sacrificing the "gentle sympathies and kindly affections" to the "intellectual all-in-all."[4]

The cult of benevolence received further impetus in the nineteenth century when the misery and degradation of industrial workers became too apparent to ignore. One way to face the growing evil was to appeal to the social conscience of the well-off, as Carlyle, Arnold, Kingsley, and Maurice did. Another was to quicken sympathy for suffering humanity. This was Dickens' way and—with a difference—George Eliot's. In an essay on Dickens, Walter Bagehot described the origin of Victorian humanitarianism:

> The unfeeling obtuseness of the early part of this century was to be corrected by an extreme—perhaps an excessive—sensibility to human suffering in the years which have followed. There was most adequate reason for the sentiment in its origin, and it had a great task to perform in ameliorating harsh customs and repealing dreadful penalties.[5]

Neither Dickens nor George Eliot was a social reformer in any positive sense. She felt that the artist's responsibility in this connection was to stimulate reform by rousing "the nobler emotions,

3. *Dissertations and Discussions, Political, Philosophical and Historical* (4 vols. London, 1875), *1*, 360.

4. *Arthur Coningsby* (London, 1833), *3*, 378; *Eustace Conway* (London, 1834), *1*, 142. I am indebted for both references, as in general for much of the material in this paragraph and the next, to W. E. Houghton, *The Victorian Frame of Mind, 1830–1870* (New Haven, 1957), pp. 263–81.

5. *Works of Walter Bagehot* (5 vols. Hartford, 1891), *2*, 269–70.

which make mankind desire the social right."[6] If men were moved to true fellow-feeling, they would inevitably promote the common good. Dickens did not aim so high, perhaps; he hoped mainly to stimulate private charity. The benevolence which he urged required simple awareness rather than sympathy. It is not necessary to go out of oneself or even to have any real understanding of another's suffering in order to obey a charitable impulse. Mr. Pickwick does not identify himself with the miserable creatures in the Fleet Prison any more than Mr. Brownlow identifies himself with Oliver Twist. Both remain just what they are—rich men in a position to help someone whose situation touches their feelings. Humphry House points out that Dickens' heroes "are all good-*natured,* and seem to act as they do because they cannot act otherwise. Not one of them has a moral policy, or a considered opinion about why he does good."[7] Without impugning either Dickens' motives or his sincerity, one may observe that this thoughtless, mechanical benevolence, based purely upon good-natured feeling, may easily degenerate into sentimentality and may, in fact, be considered a selfish indulgence. In George Eliot, sympathy is achieved through an imaginative extension of self, a thing unknown to Dickens' heroes. For her the basis of sympathy, the foundation of true benevolence, is not feeling as such but understanding.[8]

---

6. *Letters*, 7, 44. In the same letter George Eliot writes: "It is one thing to feel keenly for one's fellow-beings; another to say, 'This step, and this alone, will be the best to take for the removal of particular calamities.'"

7. *The Dickens World* (London, 1941), p. 39.

8. Cf. W. E. Houghton's comment on the difference between Dickens and George Eliot with respect to the distinction between true sympathy and simple good nature:

Benevolence need not, however, degenerate into sentimentality. It does not do so, or very slightly in the work of George Eliot, the other major Victorian besides Dickens who made its promotion a central aim of fiction. The reason is that for Eliot the essential thing, the foundation of genuine benevolence, is not feeling as such but understanding. It originates in a clear and compassionate perception of human suffering, which

Chapter Three

Finally, for George Eliot as for so many of her contemporaries, sympathy was a noble substitute for conventional religious faith. The doctrine of fellow-feeling and sympathetic action is central wherever the supernatural side of religion is felt to be weak. It enters importantly into Maurice's Christian Socialism and Kingsley's "muscular Christianity"; one thinks also of Tennyson's King Arthur and his lack of sympathy with the Grail quest, leading as he felt it did to the neglect of home duties. When the supernatural aspect of religion is denied altogether, as in the system of Auguste Comte, the doctrine of sympathy becomes paramount. George Eliot was never an orthodox adherent to Comte's system, but the fundamental precepts of the Religion of Humanity appealed strongly to one who yearned always for the old faith she had lost. Her basic agreement with one important aspect of Comte's thinking is reflected in her statement that her books

> have for their main bearing a conclusion . . . without which I could not have cared to write any representation of human life—namely, that the fellowship between man and man which has been the principle of development, social and moral, is not dependent on conceptions of what is not man: and that the idea of God, so far as it has been a high spiritual influence, is the ideal of a goodness entirely human (i.e., an exaltation of the human). (*Letters, 6, 98.*)

---

then quickens the natural emotions of pity and love; with the result that the emotions are commensurate with what such an object would normally arouse and warrant, and not, as in sentimentalism, too intense for an object which is but dimly perceived. The contrast may be made in another way that brings out the ethical difference. The sentimental indulgence of pity and love is really self-centered—one enjoys feeling a burst of kindness for those less fortunate than himself—whereas George Eliot's benevolence presupposes a forgetfulness of self in the recognition of our common humanity. The distinction meant a re-emphasis on sympathy as the power of entering into the feelings of another. *The Victorian Frame of Mind*, p. 278.

This statement, written in 1874, shows that her outlook had not changed since 1853, when she wrote to Charles Bray that the new religion, lacking the old faith that Heaven would help us, would teach us all the more to help one another. This is the distinctively Victorian basis for George Eliot's doctrine of sympathy. While the eighteenth century had acknowledged the utility of benevolence and the Romantics had insisted upon the moral importance of the sympathetic imagination, the religious doubt and the social conscience of the mid-nineteenth century made the propagation of the doctrine of sympathy, for many, a matter of grave necessity. In *Scenes of Clerical Life,* George Eliot directed her wholehearted attention to that end.

In "Amos Barton" she states her position unequivocally:

Not having a fertile imagination, as you perceive, and being unable to invent thrilling incidents for your amusement, my only merit must lie in the truth with which I represent to you the humble experience of an ordinary fellow-mortal. I wish to stir your sympathy with commonplace troubles—to win your tears for real sorrow: sorrow such as may live next door to you—such as walks neither in rags nor in velvet, but in ordinary decent apparel. (Chapter 7.)

To test to the utmost the theory implied here, she sets up as an object for sympathy as commonplace a "hero" as possible, Amos Barton: "It was not in his nature to be superlative in anything; unless, indeed, he was superlatively middling, the quintessential extract of mediocrity." (Chapter 5.) Having focused attention on such a man, describing him in naturalistic terms which prevent any sentimentalizing of the character,[9] George Eliot makes her feel-

9. "As Mr. Barton hangs up his hat in the passage, you see that a narrow face of no particular complexion—even the small-pox that has attacked it seems to have been of a mongrel, indefinite kind—with features of no particular expression, is surmounted by a slope of baldness gently rising from brow to crown." Amos has teeth which, "like the remnants of the Old Guard, were few in number, and very much the worse for wear." (Chap. 2.)

ings about him clear in an authorial aside. In connection with the apparent incongruity of the marriage between a stupid, unattractive man like Amos and so good and beautiful a woman as Milly, she says:

> But I, for one, do not grudge Amos Barton this sweet wife. I have all my life had a sympathy for mongrel ungainly dogs, who are nobody's pets; and I would rather surprise one of them by a pat and a pleasant morsel, than meet the condescending advances of the loveliest Skye-terrier who has his cushion by my lady's chair. (Chapter 2.)

Shortly after this, having implied an analogy between Amos Barton in Holy Orders and a kitchen tallow dip in a silver drawing-room candlestick, she writes:

> Alas for the worthy man who, like that candle, gets himself into the wrong place! It is only the very largest souls who will be able to appreciate and pity him—who will discern and love sincerity of purpose amid all the bungling feebleness of achievement. (Chapter 2.)

It is Amos' very lack of distinction that places the strongest claim upon our sympathies, and the opening paragraphs of Chapter 5 provide the clearest statement of George Eliot's approach to the subject. This passage, in which her theory of fiction and her doctrine of sympathy coalesce, may be taken with the opening of Chapter 17 of *Adam Bede* as the cornerstone of her artistic philosophy. She begins with the case at hand:

> The Rev. Amos Barton, whose sad fortunes I have undertaken to relate, was, you perceive, in no respect an ideal or exceptional character; and perhaps I am doing a bold thing to bespeak your sympathy on behalf of a man who was so very far from remarkable,—a man whose virtues were not heroic, and who had no undetected crime within his breast;

who had not the slightest mystery hanging about him but was palpably and unmistakably commonplace; who was not even in love, but had had that complaint favourably many years ago. "An utterly uninteresting character!" I think I hear a lady reader exclaim—Mrs. Farthingale, for example, who prefers the ideal in fiction; to whom tragedy means ermine tippets, adultery, and murder; and comedy, the adventures of some personage who is quite a "character."[1]

George Eliot enlarges upon her theme in the next paragraph and it becomes clear that the story of Amos Barton is meant to carry a significance beyond that of the specific instance:

But, my dear madam, it is so very large a majority of your fellow-countrymen that are of this insignificant stamp. At least eighty out of a hundred of your adult male fellow-Britons returned in the last census, are neither extraordinarily silly, nor extraordinarily wicked, nor extraordinarily wise; their eyes are neither deep and liquid with sentiment, nor sparkling with suppressed witticisms; they have probably had no hair-breadth escapes or thrilling adventures; their brains are certainly not pregnant with genius, and their passions have not manifested themselves at all after the fashion of a volcano. They are simply men of complexions more or less muddy, whose conversation is more or less bald and disjointed. Yet these commonplace people—many of them—bear a conscience, and have felt the sublime prompting to do the painful right; they have their unspoken sorrows, and their

---

1. The literary kinship of George Eliot and Thackeray, noted by Blackwood, is apparent in their shared distaste for the bogus in fiction. Mrs. Farthingale reminds one of the lady to whom Thackeray offered the mock-serious apology for writing about a stockbroker's family in Russell Square "without a single passionate and wonderful incident to mark the progress of their loves" when he might have written a book "supremely genteel" or "entirely low," or have "constructed a tale of thrilling interest through the fiery chapters of which the reader should hurry, panting." (*Vanity Fair,* Chap. 6.)

sacred joys; their hearts have perhaps gone out towards their first-born, and they have mourned over the irreclaimable dead. Nay, is there not a pathos in their very insignificance—in our comparison of their dim and narrow existence with the glorious possibilities of that human nature which they share?

From the half-humorous note on which this passage begins, George Eliot rises to a seriousness vibrant with humanity. From *Scenes of Clerical Life* to *Daniel Deronda* this earnest, persuasive tone is the distinctive quality of much of her authorial comment. The spirit and something of the phraseology of this passage will appear again and again in her books: "The sublime prompting to do the painful right" eloquently recalls (or anticipates) the story of Maggie Tulliver, and the final sentence of the paragraph could be put into the Prelude to *Middlemarch* without alteration. In this passage, George Eliot goes far beyond Amos Barton; for the idea here is of universal significance, a philosophical expression of far-reaching aesthetic implications. Leslie Stephen speaks of the indication found in *Scenes of Clerical Life* of a "profoundly reflective intellect, which contemplates the little dramas performed by commonplace people as parts of the wider tragi-comedy of human life."[2] The reflective, contemplative quality of George Eliot's mind is communicated directly to the reader in such a passage as this one from "Amos Barton."

It is in the choice of a "hero," then, that the doctrine of sympathy finds its first expression in "Amos Barton." The doctrine is also embodied in the story itself, which may be regarded as an illustration of the way in which sympathy—and the lack of it—affects human lives. The greatest obstacle to sympathy is selfishness, and Amos' sorrow originates in his selfishness and in that of the Countess. Hers is obvious and positive. We are told outright and we see in her actions that "there was one being to whom the Countess was absorbingly devoted, and to whose desires she made

2. *George Eliot* (New York, 1902), p. 62.

everything else subservient—namely, Caroline Czerlaski, née Bridmain." (Chapter 4.) Amos' selfishness is not of this positive sort; it is rather the negative selfishness of spiritual blindness. Unlike the Countess, he does not deliberately set out to assure his own well-being at the expense of others, but he unconsciously allows his wife to sacrifice herself to his egotism. Significantly, Amos is presented as a man almost totally lacking in imagination. He is unable to appreciate Milly because he is unable to imagine a love like hers. His lack of imagination also accounts for his inadequacy as a clergyman. This is clearly illustrated in the scene in which we see him with one of his parishioners, an old woman at the Shepperton poor-house. Seeing her seek vainly for a pinch of snuff, he says:

"So your snuff is all gone, eh?"

Mrs. Brick's eyes twinkled with the visionary hope that the parson might be intending to replenish her box, at least mediately, through the present of a small copper.

"Ah, well! you'll soon be going where there is no more snuff. You'll be in need of mercy then. You must remember that you may have to seek for mercy and not find it, just as you're seeking for snuff."

At the first sentence of this admonition, the twinkle subsided from Mrs. Brick's eyes. The lid of her box went "click!" and her heart was shut up at the same moment. (Chapter 2.)

It is not until Milly dies that Amos is brought to full recognition of his selfishness. When he returns to the empty vicarage after her funeral, he is racked by the thought that he can "never show her his love any more, never make up for omissions in the past by filling future days with tenderness." (Chapter 9.) There follows a significant interjection from the author:

O the anguish of that thought that we can never atone to our dead for the stinted affection we gave them, for the light answers we returned to their plaints or their pleadings, for the little reverence we showed to that sacred human soul that lived so close to us, and was the divinest thing God had given us to know.

It is not the thought here which is significant; that is a commonplace of human experience. But the commonplace sentiment is expressed in words which strongly suggest the religious character of George Eliot's doctrine of sympathy. The linking of "sacred" and "human," the ideas of atonement and reverence, and the implication behind the statement that knowledge of a human soul is the closest one can come to knowledge of the Divine—namely, that God exists for us most in our feeling for a fellow human being—indicate the extent to which the idea of sympathy took on a religious coloring in George Eliot's thought.

Amos Barton fails to realize the holiness of human love, and he must suffer for his blindness, and learn through his suffering. It is not enough to fulfill the minimum responsibilities inherent in the ties which bind man to man, husband to wife. One must go beyond that to a selfless recognition of the sacredness of those ties. That is the great lesson Amos learns:

Amos Barton had been an affectionate husband, and while Milly was with him, he was never visited by the thought that perhaps his sympathy with her was not quick and watchful enough; but now he re-lived all their life together, with that terrible keenness of memory and imagination which bereavement gives, and he felt as if his very love needed a pardon for its poverty and selfishness. (Chapter 9.)

As this passage makes clear, it is only when his *imagination* is at last stirred that Amos can form a true conception of love and sympathy.

The concluding sections of the story show sympathy to be the chief of what George Eliot called "those vital elements which bind men together and give a higher worthiness to their existence."[3] And "vital" is a literal description of the power of sympathy as it is displayed here. Of Mr. Cleves, a fellow clergyman, we are told:

> On the first news of Mr. Barton's calamity, he had ridden over from Tripplegate to beg that he might be made of some use, and his silent grasp of Amos's hand had penetrated like the painful thrill of life-recovering warmth to the poor be-numbed heart of the stricken man. (Chapter 9.)

And again:

> The friendly attentions, the kind pressure of the hand, the cordial looks he met with everywhere in his parish, made him feel that the fatal frost which had settled on his pastoral duties, during the Countess's residence at the Vicarage, was completely thawed, and that the hearts of his parishioners were once more open to him. (Chapter 9.)

Behind this effect lies the religious force of human sympathy: Amos, we are told, "was consecrated anew by his great sorrow."

Amos Barton learns and is presumably made better through suffering; his parishioners learn and are made better through sharing his sorrow. That sympathy is a source of the highest moral good is the thought in this paragraph describing the feeling in Shepperton when Amos' curacy is withdrawn and he is forced to move to a distant parish:

> At length the dreaded week was come, when Amos and his children must leave Shepperton. There was general regret among the parishioners at his departure: not that any one of them thought his spiritual gifts pre-eminent, or was con-

---

3. *Letters, 4,* 472. The principle behind her work, George Eliot says in this letter of 1868, is so to present "our human life as to help my readers in getting a clearer conception and a more active admiration of those vital elements which bind men together and give a higher worthiness to their existence."

scious of great edification from his ministry. But his recent troubles had called out their better sympathies, and that is always a source of love. Amos failed to touch the spring of goodness by his sermons, but he touched it effectually by his sorrows; and there was now a real bond between him and his flock. (Chapter 10.)

This passage reflects in the clearest way possible George Eliot's belief that "the idea of God, so far as it has been a high spiritual influence, is the ideal of a goodness entirely human." It is only as a man, not as a minister of God, that Amos is able to touch the spring of goodness, which is to say, bring his parishioners to God. Their sympathy with his suffering, considered as a source of love and an impulse of goodness, is an entirely human expression of God in the world, the strongest manifestation of religion in men's lives. Through this sympathy a *real* bond is forged, opposed (at least by implication) to the false or weak bond of the formal priestly relationship which had heretofore been Amos' chief claim upon his parishioners. The connection made here between suffering and sympathy, and sympathy and love is one of George Eliot's favorite themes, and it is made again in "Mr. Gilfil's Love Story" and "Janet's Repentance."

To sum up, the doctrine of sympathy operates in "Amos Barton" in three ways: the central character is deliberately chosen for his unsympathetic qualities in order to awaken sympathy where it would otherwise least likely be extended; within the story, this "hero" illustrates the suffering consequent upon a selfish failure to see the true nature of human love; and sympathy with sorrow is shown to be the best manifestation of religion in the lives of men.

The doctrine of sympathy is a less integral part of the action in "Mr. Gilfil's Love Story," finding expression mainly in the introductory chapter and in the epilogue. There is a similarity of intention behind both stories, however. In the opening chapter of the second "scene," George Eliot again imagines that some reader will object to her choice of a subject, as Mrs. Farthingale was imagined to object to Amos Barton. Having mentioned that old Mr. Gilfil is fond of "an occasional sip of gin-and-water," she says:

> Here I am aware that I have run the risk of alienating all my refined lady readers, and utterly annihilating any curiosity they may have felt to know the details of Mr. Gilfil's love story. "Gin-and-water! foh! you may as well ask us to interest ourselves in the romance of a tallow-chandler, who mingles the image of his beloved with short dips and moulds."

But as in "Amos Barton" the reader is asked to see beyond the uninteresting and commonplace surface. Gin-and-water, we are told, "like obesity, or baldness, or the gout, does not exclude a vast amount of antecedent romance":

> Alas, alas! we poor mortals are often little better than wood-ashes—there is small sign of the sap, and the leafy freshness, and the bursting buds that once were there; but wherever we see wood-ashes we know that all that early fulness of life must have been. I, at least, hardly ever look at a bent old man, or a wizened old woman, but I see also, with my mind's eye, that Past of which they are the shrunken remnant, and the unfinished romance of rosy cheeks and bright eyes seems sometimes of feeble interest and significance, compared with that drama of hope and love which has long ago reached its catastrophe, and left the poor soul, like a dim and dusty stage, with all its sweet garden-scenes and fair perspectives over-turned and thrust out of sight.[4]

In the Epilogue, George Eliot returns to the theme of this passage to reflect upon the proposition set up here and illustrated

---

4. This passage anticipates in an interesting way Arnold Bennett's familiar description of the inspiration of *The Old Wives' Tale* (1908). See the preface

in the story proper, which shows the "passion and the poetry" that a sympathetic imagination sees beneath the ordinary surface of life. The Epilogue, which with the introductory chapter encloses the main action in an envelope of reflective comment, is much the best part of the story; one is more moved by the affectionate description of the old vicar than by the rather contrived pathos of his love story. In the Epilogue George Eliot's sympathy comes into full play. She had first intended to end the story with the death of Caterina, and the Epilogue was an afterthought.[5] It was meant primarily to soften the pathos of the ending, but it also provided an opportunity for stating an idea fundamental to the doctrine of sympathy—namely, that we often misjudge others because of our imperfect understanding of them. The Epilogue begins:

> This was Mr. Gilfil's love-story, which lay far back from the time when he sat, worn and grey, by his lonely fireside in Shepperton Vicarage. Rich brown locks, passionate love and deep early sorrow, strangely different as they seem from the scanty white hairs, the apathetic content, and the unexpectant quiescence of old age, are but part of the same life's journey; as the bright Italian plains, with the sweet *Addio* of their beckoning maidens, are part of the same day's travel that brings us to the other side of the mountain, between the sombre rocky walls and among the guttural voices of the Valais.

The idea is developed further, with a return to the sap and leaf imagery of Chapter 1, in the next paragraph. Acknowledging that

---

to that novel, where Bennett tells of his glimpse of a grotesque old woman who "in the long lapse of years . . . had developed the kind of peculiarity which induces guffaws among the thoughtless," and of his preoccupation with the thought that "this woman was once young, slim, perhaps beautiful."

5. See *Letters*, 2, 324 and note.

"the Mr. Gilfil of those late Shepperton days had more of the knots and ruggedness of poor human nature than there lay any clear hint of in the open-eyed loving Maynard" of forty years before, the narrator adds:

> But it is with men as with trees: if you lop off their finest branches, into which they were pouring their young life-juice, the wounds will be healed over with some rough boss, some odd excrescence; and what might have been a grand tree expanding into liberal shade, is but a whimsical misshapen trunk.

This reflection, so exactly descriptive of the particular case at hand—the whimsical, crusty old vicar who had been young Gilfil "with a heart full of passion and tenderness"—is expanded into a moral observation in which we observe the understanding, tolerant view of life which is associated with George Eliot's work. Nothing in the human condition, she seems to say, is beyond explanation and nothing beyond sympathy:

> Many an irritating fault, many an unlovely oddity has come of a hard sorrow, which has crushed and maimed the nature just when it was expanding into plenteous beauty; and the trivial erring life which we visit with our harsh blame, may be but as the unsteady motion of a man whose best limb is withered.

Thus, Mr. Gilfil's story, like Amos Barton's, is meant to widen the sympathies of the reader. The old man is another of those commonplace people who have "their unspoken sorrows, and their sacred joys," another subject for the moral exercise of learning to see "the poetry and the pathos, the tragedy and the comedy, lying in the experience of a human soul that looks out through dull grey eyes, and that speaks in a voice of quite ordinary tones."

This story differs from "Amos Barton" in that it asks for understanding rather than for pity. In a broad sense, the Epilogue to "Mr. Gilfil's Love Story" is a gentle plea for tolerance, for not sitting in judgment on our fellow men, of whom we can have but imperfect knowledge. The case for charity is stated in the main part of the story also, though with a rather special application, for it comes when Gilfil is attempting to dispel Caterina's sense of guilt about Wybrow's death. His words have a broader significance, however, in that they embody a significant concept of the doctrine of sympathy:

> "We mean to do wicked things that we never could do, just as we mean to do good or clever things that we never could do. Our thoughts are often worse than we are, just as they are often better than we are. And God sees us as we are altogether, not in separate feelings or actions as our fellow-men see us. We are always doing each other injustice, and thinking better or worse of each other than we deserve, because we only hear and see separate words and actions. We don't see each other's whole nature." (Chapter 19.)

Shortly after this he says: "If we knew ourselves, we should not judge each other harshly." The religious nature of human love and the value of shared suffering are also brought out in connection with Gilfil's efforts to help Caterina:

> Mr. Gilfil felt as if in the long hours of that night the bond that united his love for ever and alone to Caterina had acquired fresh strength and sanctity. It is so with the human relations that rest on the deep emotional sympathy of affection: every new day and night of joy or sorrow is a new consecration. (Chapter 19.)

Sorrow, sympathy, love, consecration—these are the key words in George Eliot's view of human affection, and it is with these things that *Scenes of Clerical Life* deals.

In "Janet's Repentance" the doctrine of sympathy receives its fullest expression. The story of Janet Dempster's degradation and redemption and of Mr. Tryan's self-sacrifice gives a more direct demonstration of sympathy in action than is found in the other two "scenes." In "Amos Barton" to some extent and almost entirely in "Mr. Gilfil's Love Story," the expression of the idea is mainly purposive—it gives meaning to the action but the action itself, considered purely as narrative material, is concerned with something else. In "Janet's Repentance" the plot is in itself a dramatization of the idea.

In her presentation of Mr. Tryan, George Eliot has created an Evangelical clergyman of the highest type. Evangelicalism, however, is too narrow a term to encompass the elements of his religion. Without falsifying the Evangelical background, which is an important part of the social realism in her picture of Milby, George Eliot embodies in Mr. Tryan ideals which are above sectarian description. He is unmistakably and believably Evangelical, but his religion is essentially a religion of humanity; he has the characteristic Evangelical beliefs and expresses them in the characteristic manner, but it is through a doctrine of sympathy purely human that Janet is saved. George Eliot emphasized to Blackwood that the "collision in the drama is not at all between 'bigotted churchmanship' and evangelicalism, but between *ir*religion and religion." (*Letters, 2,* 347.) And by religion she means morality: "I thought I had made it apparent . . . that the conflict lay between immorality and morality—irreligion and religion." (*Letters, 2,* 347.)

Among the principal elements in George Eliot's novels Basil Willey has noted "the supersession of God by Humanity, of Faith by Love and Sympathy, the elimination of the supernatural, the elevation of the natural, the subordination of intellect to heart, thought to feeling."[6] Several passages in "Janet's Repentance"

6. *Nineteenth Century Studies,* p. 237.

are of particular interest for the light they shed on the last aspect of her work mentioned here. One of the most striking instances comes at the turning point of Janet's life when, having been driven from home by her husband and feeling her life altogether desolate, she turns as a last resort to Mr. Tryan. At the conclusion of a long interview in which Tryan succeeds in giving Janet hope and comfort, George Eliot writes:

> Blessed influence of one true loving human soul on another! Not calculable by algebra, not deducible by logic, but mysterious, effectual, mighty as the hidden process by which the tiny seed is quickened, and bursts forth into tall stem and broad leaf, and glowing tasselled flower. Ideas are often poor ghosts; our sun-filled eyes cannot discern them; they pass athwart us in thin vapour, and cannot make themselves felt. But sometimes they are made flesh; they breathe upon us with warm breath, they touch us with soft responsive hands, they look at us with sad sincere eyes, and speak to us in appealing tones; they are clothed in a living human soul, with all its conflicts, its faith, and its love. Then their presence is a power, then they shake us like a passion, and we are drawn after them with gentle compulsion, as flame is drawn to flame. (Chapter 19.)

In effect, it is not Mr. Tryan's specific religious belief that touches Janet but his humanity. Ideas are important—"their presence is a power"—but only when they are informed by feeling. "I have had heart-cutting experience that opinions are a poor cement between human souls," George Eliot once wrote to Charles Bray (*Letters*, 3, 111), and that is the thought of this passage. For "opinions" may be substituted "doctrines," and the relevance becomes even more apparent. Mr. Tryan says many things to Janet, conventional things about God's wisdom and the frailty of man, but it is his presence rather than his words that comforts her.

An even stronger statement of the ascendancy of the heart over the intellect is made later in the story when George Eliot pauses in the narrative to reflect on the importance of the individual as distinct from mankind in the mass:

> It is probably a hard saying to the Pharisees, that "there is more joy in heaven over one sinner that repenteth, than over ninety and nine just persons that need no repentance." And certain ingenious philosophers of our own day must surely take offence at a joy so entirely out of correspondence with arithmetical proportion. But a heart that has been taught by its own sore struggles to bleed for the woes of another— that has "learned pity through suffering"—is likely to find very imperfect satisfaction in the "balance of happiness," "doctrine of compensation," and other short and easy methods of obtaining thorough complacency in the presence of pain; and for such a heart that saying will not be altogether dark. (Chapter 22.)

As is so often the case when one begins to look for George Eliot's personal philosophy in her fiction, her letters furnish a text for discussion. In November 1857, she wrote to Mr. Bray, concerning a passage from *The Philosophy of Necessity* which Sara Hennell had quoted in *Christianity and Infidelity:*

> I dislike extremely a passage quoted by Sara in which you appear to consider the disregard of individuals as a lofty condition of mind. My own experience and development deepen every day my conviction that our moral progress may be measured by the degree in which we sympathize with individual suffering and individual joy. (*Letters, 2, 403.*)

Had Mr. Bray read "Janet's Repentance" and known who George Eliot was, he could not have been unprepared for this letter. The mistake of the "ingenious philosophers"—Bentham and the Utilitarians, of whom Mr. Bray was one—with their theories of the greatest good for the greatest number, lies in separating thought from feeling. In "Janet's Repentance" George Eliot stresses the thought that intellect without emotion can promulgate only false doctrine, easily refuted by the facts of human experience:

> The emotions, I have observed, are but slightly influenced by arithmetical considerations: the mother, when her sweet lisping little ones have all been taken from her one after another, and she is hanging over her last dead babe, finds small consolation in the fact that the tiny dimpled corpse is but one of a necessary average, and that a thousand other babes brought into the world at the same time are doing well, and are likely to live; and if you stood beside that mother— if you knew her pang and shared it—it is probable you would be equally unable to see a ground of complacency in statistics. (Chapter 22.)

Here is the claim of the moral imagination: "If you knew her pang and shared it"—this is the point to which George Eliot always returns in any discussion of morality. Those who base their moral philosophy only on statistics she treats with contemptuous irony:

> Doubtless a complacency resting on that basis is highly rational; but emotion, I fear, is obstinately irrational: it insists on caring for individuals; it absolutely refuses to adopt the quantitative view of human anguish, and to admit that thirteen happy lives are a set-off against twelve miserable lives, which leaves a clear balance on the side of satisfaction. This is the inherent imbecility of feeling, and one must be a great philosopher to have got quite clear of all that, and to have emerged into the serene air of pure intellect, in which it is evident that individuals really exist for no other purpose than that abstractions may be drawn from them—abstractions that may rise from heaps of ruined lives like the sweet savour

of a sacrifice in the nostrils of philosophers, and of a philo-
sophic Deity. (Chapter 22.)

George Eliot had made her feelings about the "quantitative
view of human anguish" clear in a passage which appears in the
manuscript of "Mr. Gilfil's Love Story" but not in the published
version:

> But who can measure pain? Who can fix the value of a single
> human consciousness? If human thought in an attempt to
> grasp the universal, learns to think the anguish of one living
> being trivial, this is only because human love is feeble, and
> human wisdom narrow. (MS fol. 90.)

It is interesting to speculate as to George Eliot's reasons for not
publishing this. Possibly she wanted to reserve the thought for
fuller treatment in "Janet's Repentance." Or she may have felt
the reflection overly weighty to be placed in the midst of Caterina's
troubles. Or again, as the lines would have stood at the end of
Chapter 5, it may be simply that she preferred the wistful note on
which the chapter, as published, ends. In any case, as "Janet's
Repentance" shows, it cannot have been because she did not believe in the idea expressed.

The importance of thinking of human beings as individuals is
stressed again with reference to Mr. Tryan. In a long aside on
Evangelicalism, George Eliot analyzes the type of the Evangelical
preacher, concluding with the acknowledgment that the "bird's-
eye glance of the critic" will make Mr. Tryan "the text for a wise
discourse on the characteristics of the Evangelical school in his
day." (Chapter 10.) But the mind uninformed by the sympathetic
imagination which alone can bring one man close to another is
bound to reach wrong conclusions. George Eliot wishes to bring
the reader to her own point of view: "I am on the level and in the
press with him, as he struggles his way along the stony road,
through the crowd of unloving fellow-men." When at last he

falls, the coldly classifying mind of the critic, failing to see his value as an individual, dismisses him: " 'Not a remarkable specimen; the anatomy and habits of his species have been determined long ago.' " But behind the doctrines and opinions which provide the labels for men is the individual, and man's importance as an individual transcends classification:

> Surely, surely the only true knowledge of our fellow-man is that which enables us to feel with him—which gives us a fine ear for the heart-pulses that are beating under the mere clothes of circumstance and opinion. Our subtlest analysis of schools and sects must miss the essential truth, unless it be lit up by the love that sees in all forms of human thought and work, the life and death struggles of separate human beings. (Chapter 10.)

Clearly this is one of the main points which George Eliot wanted to make in "Janet's Repentance."

A second aspect of the doctrine of sympathy that finds full expression in the story has to do with the value of suffering. What was implied in "Amos Barton" and "Mr. Gilfil's Love Story" is made explicit in "Janet's Repentance." At the end of the passage in which George Eliot refutes the statistical philosophy of happiness she writes:

> And so it comes to pass that for the man who knows sympathy because he has known sorrow, that old, old saying about the joy of angels over the repentant sinner outweighing their joy over the ninety-nine just, has a meaning which does not jar with the language of his own heart. It only tells him that for angels too there is a transcendent value in human pain, which refuses to be settled by equations. (Chapter 22.)

The value in human pain is twofold. First, through our own experience of pain we learn to sympathize with the pain of others:

82

it is only the "heart that has been taught by its own sore struggles to bleed for the woes of another" that can achieve true sympathy. One must therefore have suffered to be able to sympathize. The second value of pain is that it gives a man an opportunity to enter into an active sympathetic relationship with his fellows. Both ideas find direct expression in Ludwig Feuerbach's *Das Wesen Christenthums,* which George Eliot had translated in 1854. "Love does not exist without sympathy, sympathy does not exist without suffering in common,"[7] Feuerbach asserts. This concept persisted in George Eliot's thinking even after the intellectual radicalism which had found Feuerbach's doctrines so congenial had passed its peak.

The idea of suffering as a value is embodied in the relationship between Janet and Mr. Tryan. "Mr. Tryan," we are told, "had gone through the initiation of suffering: it is no wonder, then, that Janet's restoration was the work that lay nearest his heart." (Chapter 22.) And it is because he has suffered himself that he feels he can be of use to Janet:

> He saw that the first thing Janet needed was to be assured of sympathy. She must be made to feel that her anguish was not strange to him; that he entered into the only half-expressed secrets of her spiritual weakness, before any other message of consolation could find its way to her heart. The tale of the Divine Pity was never yet believed from lips that were not felt to be moved by human pity. And Janet's anguish was not strange to Mr. Tryan. He had never been in the presence of a sorrow and a self-despair that had sent so strong a thrill through all the recesses of his saddest experience; and it is because sympathy is but a living again through our own past in a new form, that confession often prompts a response of confession. (Chapter 18.)

7. *The Essence of Christianity,* Eng. trans. Marian Evans (London, 1854), p. 53.

Therefore he tells her that he speaks as a "fellow-sinner who has needed just the comfort and help you are needing," and when she begs him for some assurance of hope, he says: "Yes, dear Mrs. Dempster . . . there *is* comfort, there *is* hope for you. Believe me there is, for I speak from my own deep and hard experience." (Chapter 18.) His "initiation in suffering" came when a young girl whom he had seduced in his college days subsequently became a prostitute and ultimately committed suicide. This typically Victorian bit of melodrama was hackneyed even when it was written,[8] and the fact that George Eliot could make it a part of her story indicates how important she felt it to be to give some concrete evidence of Mr. Tryan's being a fellow sufferer with Janet. The essential strength of their relationship lies in the fact that he can sympathize fully because he has suffered as deeply, that he can tell her that he has been in a "state of self-reproach and despair, which enables me to understand to the full what you are suffering." (Chapter 18.) He can, in other words, make that imaginative identification upon which the fullest sympathy depends.

Janet's reason for sending for Mr. Tryan is significantly related to the concept of suffering embodied in the story. Her only previous direct contact with him had been at the house of a dying girl whom she had gone to visit. Entering the house without knocking, she overhears Mr. Tryan talking to the girl, asking her to pray from him in his trials. Janet is astonished that there is about the Evangelical preacher "none of the self-satisfied unction of the teacher, quoting, exhorting, or expounding, for the benefit of the hearer, but a simple appeal for help, a confession of weakness":

Mr. Tryan had his deeply-felt troubles, then? Mr. Tryan, too, like herself, knew what it was to tremble at a foreseen

---

8. Blackwood apparently complained of this. In a letter to the publisher, Lewes wrote: "What you say about the hackneyed nature of the clergyman's story is perfectly true." (*Letters, 2,* 378.) Blackwood's letter has not been found but there can be no doubt that he referred to this part of the story.

trial—to shudder at an impending burthen, heavier than he felt able to bear?

The most brilliant deed of virtue could not have inclined Janet's good-will towards Mr. Tryan so much as this fellow-ship in suffering. (Chapter 12.)

Thus, it is not surprising that when Janet is in the deepest despair she thinks of Mr. Tryan as of one with whom she has a "fellow-ship in suffering": "That short interview with Mr. Tryan had come back upon her—his voice, his words, his look, which told her that he knew sorrow." (Chapter 16.)

The "transcendent value" of the personal experience of pain, then, is that it enables us to enter more fully into the sorrow of others. The value of the pain of others is that it gives us an opportunity to sympathize with sorrow outside ourselves and thus to realize the highest possibilities of our nature. What we transcend in sympathizing with another's pain is made clear in the passage describing Janet's vigil at the bedside of her dying husband. The passage is also another indication of the subordination of intellect to heart in the story:

Within the four walls where the stir and glare of the world are shut out, and every voice is subdued—where a human being lies prostrate, thrown on the tender mercies of his fellow, the moral relation of man to man is reduced to its utmost clearness and simplicity: bigotry cannot confuse it, theory cannot pervert it, passion, awed into quiescence, can neither pollute nor perturb it. As we bend over the sick-bed, all the forces of our nature rush towards the channels of pity, of patience, and of love, and sweep down the miserable choking drift of our quarrels, our debates, our would-be wisdom, and our clamorous selfish desires. This blessing of serene freedom from the importunities of opinion lies in all simple direct acts of mercy. (Chapter 24.)

Chapter Three

Of all that man transcends in sympathizing with the suffering of another, it is his own egotism and his "clamorous selfish desires" which in the first place are most likely to prove obstacles to genuine fellow-feeling. George Eliot, therefore, makes selflessness the goal towards which Janet moves in her struggle for redemption. In the early part of the story the selfishness of her despair is emphasized. Janet has great pride and this forces her to present a calm front to the world, but we are told, "When the sun had sunk, and the twilight was deepening, Janet might be . . . heated, maddened, sobbing out her griefs with selfish passion, and wildly wishing herself dead." (Chapter 5.) Later we see her doing just this:

> "Mother! why don't you speak to me?" Janet burst out at last; "you don't care about my suffering; you are blaming me because I feel—because I am miserable. . . . You don't ask me what it is I have had to bear. You are tired of hearing me. You are cruel, like the rest; every one is cruel in this world. Nothing but blame—blame—blame; never any pity. God is cruel to have sent me into the world to bear all this misery." (Chapter 14.)

After the interview with Mr. Tryan, Janet is able to see herself clearly, and she sees that selfishness is at the bottom of her misery: "I have been thinking only of myself," she tells him. "I was only angry and discontented because I had pain to bear." Henceforth she works out her redemption by devoting her life to others: "Life to her could never more have any eagerness; it was a solemn service of gratitude and patient effort." (Chapter 28.)

This had also been the way to salvation for Mr. Tryan, the greatest examplar of unselfishness in the story. Self-sacrifice is the theme of his life. His physical weakness, emphasized even before he appears in the story, is a constant cause for concern among his followers:

86

The Doctrine of Sympathy

"I wonder if there's another man in the world who has been brought up as Mr. Tryan has, that would choose to live in those small rooms on the common, among heaps of dirty cottages, for the sake of being near the poor people," said Mrs. Pettifer. "I'm afraid he hurts his health by it; he looks to me far from strong." (Chapter 3.)

"Self-denial," "self-privation," and "self-mortification" are terms used over and over in connection with Mr. Tryan, and his selflessness extends to the utmost limit. When one of his friends remonstrates with him about the way in which he drives himself—"Isn't it a'most a-killin' o' yourself, to go on a' that way beyond your strength?"—and tells him that "We mustn't fling our lives away," Mr. Tryan answers: "No, not fling them away lightly, but we are permitted to lay down our lives in a right cause. There are many duties, as you know, Mr. Jerome, which stand before taking care of our own lives." (Chapter 11.) One of the duties which stands before the taking care of his own life is Janet's redemption. When he first feels that he has made some progress towards her salvation, he is described as "an image of . . . self-renouncing faith" and his prayer is: "Let me only live to see this work confirmed." (Chapter 19.) Mr. Tryan's selflessness is set forth in "Janet's Repentance" as the best evidence of Divine Love in human life. "The first condition of human goodness is something to love," George Eliot writes, "the second, something to reverence. And this latter precious gift was brought to Milby by Mr. Tryan and Evangelicalism." (Chapter 10.)

Apart from providing the major themes of the story, the doctrine of sympathy finds expression again and again in "Janet's Repentance" in casual phrases and passing bits of characterization. It is the basis for the portrait of Mr. Jerome, for instance, an old farmer who is presented as the epitome of simple goodness, a man whose philosophy of life is paraphrased thus: "Ah, friends, this pleasant world is a sad one, too, isn't it? Let us help one another, let us help one another." (Chapter 8.) Mr. Jerome "drew the elements of his moral vision from the depths of his veneration and pity," we are told (Chapter 11), and "The sympathy of this simple-minded old man was more precious to Mr. Tryan than any mere onlooker could have imagined." (Chapter 8.) Even in the picture of the brutal Dempster sympathy plays a part. Dempster is George Eliot's first crude attempt to portray moral deterioration, one of the things for which she is most highly praised in her later work. She herself pointed out to Blackwood what she was striving for in the characterization: "Dempster's vices have their natural evolution in deeper and deeper moral deterioration." (*Letters, 2,* 347.) But even Dempster, we are told—and one notes that here as throughout the *Scenes* the imagery of moral goodness is drawn from the processes of natural growth—feels "those stirrings of the more kindly, healthy sap of human feeling, by which goodness tries to get the upper hand in us whenever it seems to have the slightest chance," and in his kindness to his old mother we see "how hard it is to kill the deep-down fibrous roots of human love and goodness—how the man from whom we make it our pride to shrink, has yet a close brotherhood with us in some of our most sacred feelings." (Chapter 7.)

The sacred quality of human sympathy is a recurrent concept in "Janet's Repentance." When Janet is turned out of her home she is taken in by her friend, Mrs. Pettifer, who puts her to bed and comforts her. Janet's kisses of gratitude for this act of kindness are said to be "sacramental kisses—such kisses as seal a new and closer bond between the helper and the helped." (Chapter 15.) The kiss which Janet gives Mr. Tryan on his deathbed is "a sacred kiss of promise." (Chapter 27.) Janet's bond with Mrs. Pettifer and her sympathetic relationship with Mr. Tryan are sacramental in themselves, expressive of the highest religious significance. Human sympathy is sacred because it is the means by which we come to understand Divine sympathy. Two sentences from "Janet's Repentance" show this to be a part of George Eliot's thought.

One (quoted above on page 83) occurs in the description of Mr. Tryan's first long talk with Janet: "The tale of Divine Pity was never yet believed from lips that were not felt to be moved by human pity." (Chapter 18.) The thought is stated even more explicitly later when Janet goes to Mr. Tryan after having nearly given in to the old temptation of drink: "The act of confiding in human sympathy, the consciousness that a fellow-being was listening to her with patient pity, prepared her soul for that stronger leap by which faith grasps the idea of the Divine sympathy." (Chapter 25.) And her soul does make the leap. As Janet walks home through the night, she experiences the sense of salvation:

> That walk in the dewy starlight remained for ever in Janet's memory as one of those baptismal epochs, when the soul, dipped in the sacred waters of joy and peace, rises from them with new energies, with more unalterable longings. (Chapter 25.)

This is the moment of Janet's redemption; it is significantly Wordsworthian in its nature. The "sacred waters of joy and peace" are the streams of human sympathy. The connection is easy to make for the imagery here has been used before. When Janet was deepest in despair she had thought of her life as "a sun-dried, barren tract, where there was no shadow, and where all the waters were bitter," (Chapter 16) and when her thoughts turn to Mr. Tryan, the remembrance of him is the "one spot in her memory which seemed to promise her an untried spring, where the waters might be sweet." "His words come to me," she tells her mother later, "like rain on the parched ground." (Chapter 20.) The imagery applies to Mr. Tryan's feelings, too. The bond with Janet is as significant for him as for her, and he yearns for "a draught of that deep affection from which he had been cut off by a dark chasm of remorse"; he thinks of that affection as "a palm-shadowed well in the desert." (Chapter 27.) Thus, sympathy is presented as the life-giving water indispensable to human existence. This, one may say in conclusion, is the primary theme of George Eliot's first work of fiction, the chief of those ideas about which she cared "a good deal," and for which she valued *Scenes of Clerical Life* as an embodiment.

Richard Niebuhr has said that George Eliot "sought to retain the ethos of Christianity without its faith, its humanism without its theism."[9] The accuracy of this observation is demonstrated everywhere in *Scenes of Clerical Life.* The doctrine of sympathy embodied in the work is obviously Christian in its essential points, but it is the practical side of Christian ethics that is expressed. It is the love of man, not the love of God, that is taught here. God is mentioned in these stories, of course, because they are stories about people who believe in God in a perfectly conventional sense. But if every reference to God were taken out, the essential message of the book would be unchanged: "Ah, friends, this pleasant world is a sad one, too, isn't it? Let us help one another, let us help one another." This view may lead one to a God answering doctrinal descriptions, and George Eliot has that "negative capability" which enables her to understand and portray those who feel that it has done so in their lives. But this is a secondary effect, and her conception of religion remains firmly based in humanity.

George Eliot's moral philosophy is nowhere expressed more clearly than in *Scenes of Clerical Life.* For this very reason, perhaps, it is not in the expression of the doctrine of sympathy that her genius as a novelist is best indicated in her first work of fiction. The sympathy is too self-conscious. As the quotations in this discussion show, it is mainly through authorial comment that George Eliot's sympathy operates in these stories; the imaginative insight which manifests itself in the creation of characters who

9. Introduction to Feuerbach, *The Essence of Christianity* (New York, 1957), p. ix.

can call forth sympathy in and of themselves is only just emerging here. But *Scenes of Clerical Life* is not without other indications that the author will go on to greater things. For such indications one turns from the doctrine of sympathy, in which we see George Eliot the moralist, to the humor and pathos of "Amos Barton," the melodrama of "Mr. Gilfil's Love Story," and the realism of "Janet's Repentance," in which we see George Eliot the artist.

4. EXPERIMENTS IN NARRATIVE

"AMOS BARTON": HUMOR AND PATHOS

When "Amos Barton" first appeared, it was praised most for its humor and pathos. Today the primary interest of the story derives rather from those passages which express so clearly George Eliot's theory of fiction and her doctrine of sympathy, for from these one may draw important generalizations about her approach to the art of fiction. But considered as "prentice-work" (to use F. R. Leavis' term for the *Scenes*), it is still in her treatment of the humorous and the pathetic elements that we see most plainly the literary craftsmanship of the beginning novelist. For a novelist whose professed aim was to depict the tragedy and the comedy of ordinary life, nothing could be more important than the ability to re-create the humor and pathos in the lives of simple people. "Amos Barton" permitted George Eliot to test her abilities in this respect.

The humor in "Amos Barton" is best when George Eliot writes with mild irony. She displays a gift for terse, dry characterization that recalls Jane Austen while at the same time anticipating her own great success in this manner in subsequent novels. As the shadow of Milly's death lengthens over the story, the humorous

93

and ironic element naturally disappears, for the last chapters are pure pathos and tenderness; in the earlier sections, however, George Eliot gives free rein to her sense of the comic, and the first four chapters are rich in ironic characterization. Perhaps the best example of this is the scene in Chapter 1 which first convinced Lewes that George Eliot could write good dialogue.

In this passage, we are introduced to several of Amos Barton's parishioners who are gathered at Cross Farm around the fireside of Mrs. Patten, "a childless old lady, who had got rich chiefly by the negative process of spending nothing." Pouring tea is Mrs. Patten's niece, "a single lady of fifty, who had refused the most ineligible offers out of devotion to her aged aunt." Mrs. Patten is described neatly and with wit:

> Quiescence in an easy-chair, under the sense of compound interest perpetually accumulating, has long seemed an ample function to her, and she does her malevolence gently. She is a pretty little old woman of eighty, with a close cap and tiny flat white curls round her face, as natty and unsoiled and invariable as the waxen image of a little old lady under a glass-case; once a lady's-maid, and married for her beauty. She used to adore her husband, and now she adores her money, cherishing a quiet blood-relation's hatred for her niece, Janet Gibbs, who, she knows, expects a large legacy, and whom she is determined to disappoint. Her money shall all go in a lump to a distant relation of her husband's and Janet shall be saved the trouble of pretending to cry, by finding that she is left with a miserable pittance.

This description is not simply amusing in itself; it is an integral part of the presentation of Mrs. Patten's character. All her subsequent speeches are made consistent and believable by reference to the egoism, vanity, and malice implied here. The passage also establishes the relationship between aunt and niece so clearly that we hardly need to be told further on that "Janet seemed always to identify herself with her aunt's personality, holding her own under protest." The following exchange, later in the story, comes as an amusing confirmation of the relationship described here:

"Well!" remarked Miss Gibbs, "if I was a wife, nothing should induce me to bear what Mrs. Barton does."

"Yes, it's fine talking," said Mrs. Patten, from her pillow; "old maids' husbands are al'ys well-managed. If you was a wife you'd be as foolish as your betters, belike." (Chapter 6.)

Mrs. Patten's guests in this scene are her neighbors, Mr. and Mrs. Hackit, and her doctor, Mr. Pilgrim. The irony prevails in the description of Mrs. Hackit and the doctor. Mr. Pilgrim is a man who, "though occasionally affecting aristocratic airs, and giving late dinners with enigmatic side-dishes and poisonous port, is never so comfortable as when he is relaxing his professional legs in one of those excellent farmhouses where the mice are sleek and the mistress sickly." The last part of this description demonstrates George Eliot's comic talent for joining words or ideas in unexpected ways. This may be observed all through "Amos Barton," in casual phrases as in the description of the "very dyspeptic and evangelical" Mr. Duke and the "transcendental and nearsighted" Mr. Baird (Chapter 6), as well as in whole sentences: " 'I used to think Barton was only a fool,' observed Mr. Pilgrim, in a tone which implied that he was conscious of having been weakly charitable." (Chapter 6.) This manner is well illustrated in the description of Mrs. Hackit:

Mrs. Hackit declines cream; she has so long abstained from it with an eye to the weekly butter-money, that abstinence, wedded to habit, has begotten aversion. She is a thin woman with a chronic liver-complaint, which would have secured her Mr. Pilgrim's entire regard and unreserved good word, even if he had not been in awe of her tongue, which was as sharp as his own lancet. She has brought her knitting—no

95

frivolous fancy knitting, but a subtantial woollen stocking; the click-click of her knitting-needles is the running accompaniment to all her conversation, and in her utmost enjoyment of spoiling a friend's self-satisfaction, she was never known to spoil a stocking. (Chapter 1.)

As in the case of Mrs. Patten and Mr. Pilgrim, the first description fixes Mrs. Hackit's character quite definitely, and the consistency of the portrait is a source of pleasure in the subsequent development. Her downright air of no-nonsense is apparent when she stands forth as sole defender of Amos Barton:

"Well," said Mrs. Hackit, whose good-nature began to act now that it was a little in contradiction with the dominant tone of the conversation, "*I* like Mr. Barton. I think he's a good sort o' man, for all he's not overburthen'd i' th' upper story."

Having come to know Mrs. Hackit so well at first meeting, it is with amusement but not surprise that we learn much later in the story that

Mrs. Hackit regulated her costume by the calendar, and brought out her furs on the first of November, whatever might be the temperature. She was not a woman weakly to accommodate herself to shilly-shally proceedings. If the season didn't know what it ought to do, Mrs. Hackit did. In her best days, it was always sharp weather at "Gunpowder Plot," and she didn't like new fashions.[1] (Chapter 6.)

The good-humored satire of the passage is reinforced when George Eliot continues, "and this morning the weather was very rationally

1. Mrs. Hackit's attitude toward the weather recalls another strong-minded woman, Lady Catherine de Bourgh, who assembled the party at Rosings in the evening to tell them what the next day's weather would be (*Pride and Prejudice,* Chap. 29). Mrs. Hackit's approach to dates recalls a statement in George Eliot's article on Riehl: "The peculiarity of the peasant's language consists

in accordance with her costume." There follows a description of the November morning, which leads to lines suggesting a kinship between Mrs. Hackit and Mrs. Poyser in *Adam Bede,* and shows already developed George Eliot's knack for homespun epigrammatic speech:

> "Ah," Mrs. Hackit thought to herself, "I dare say we shall have a sharp pinch this winter, and if we do, I shouldn't wonder if it takes the old lady off. They say a green Yule makes a fat churchyard; but so does a white Yule too, for that matter. When the stool's rotten enough, no matter who sits on't."

It is worth noting that every word in this passage, with the single exception of "matter," is of Anglo-Saxon origin. This great preponderance of native vocabulary is characteristic of the speech of all the farm people in *Scenes of Clerical Life,* and contributes much to our sense of the reality of the Shepperton world.

The other member of the group at Cross Farm, Mr. Hackit, is presented without irony. At least, no irony is directed at him, although in describing him George Eliot glances ironically at Mrs. Patten:

> Mrs. Patten has more respect for her neighbour Mr. Hackit than for most people. Mr. Hackit is a shrewd substantial man, whose advice about crops is always worth listening to, and who is too well off to want to borrow money. (Chapter 1.)

The humor of "Amos Barton" does not lie solely in the descriptions, however. The speech of Mr. Hackit, for instance, occasional-

---

chiefly in his retention of historical peculiarities, which gradually disappear under the friction of cultivated circles. He prefers any proper name that may be given to a day in the calendar, rather than the abstract date, by which he very rarely reckons." (*WR,* 66 [July 1856], 59.)

ly suggests the racy idiom and forthright, uneducated reasonableness of the justly admired rustics in *Silas Marner:*

> "I've heard the Ranters out o' doors in Yorkshire go on for an hour or two on end, without ever sticking fast a minute. There was one clever chap, I remember, as used to say, 'You're like the wood-pigeon; it says do, do, do all day, and never sets about any work itself.' That's bringing it home to people. But our parson's no gift at all that way; he can preach as good a sermon as need be heard when he writes it down. But when he tries to preach wi'out book, he rambles about, and doesn't stick to his text; and every now and then he flounders about like a sheep as has cast itself, and can't get on'ts legs again." (Chapter 1.)

And later in the story:

> "I never seen the like to parsons," Mr. Hackit said one day in conversation with his brother churchwarden, Mr. Bond; "They're al'ys for meddlin' wi' business, an' they know no moor about it than my black filly."
>
> "Ah," said Mr. Bond, "They're too high learnt to have much common-sense."
>
> "Well," remarked Mr. Hackit, in a modest and dubious tone, as if throwing out a hypothesis which might be considered bold, "I should say that's a bad sort o' eddication as makes folks unreasonable." (Chapter 5.)

Such speeches as these are distinctively George Eliot's creation; they exploit the rustic mentality as a source of amusement, while at the same time bringing the reader to a sympathetic understanding of the countryman's outlook. This method of pleasing while instructing may also be observed in the following speech of Mrs. Patten's:

"Eh, dear," said Mrs. Patten, falling back in her chair, and lifting up her little withered hands, "what 'ud Mr. Gilfil say, if he was worthy to know the changes as have come about i' the church these last ten years? I don't understand these new sort o' doctrines. When Mr. Barton comes to see me, he talks about nothing but my sins and my need o' marcy. Now, Mr. Hackit, I've never been a sinner. From the fust beginning, when I went into service, I al'ys did my duty by my emplyers. I was a good wife as any in the county—never aggravated my husband. The cheese-factor used to say my cheeses was al'ys to be depended on. I've known women, as their cheese swelled a shame to be seen, when their husbands had counted on the cheese-money to make up their rent; and yet they'd three gowns to my one. If I'm not to be saved, I know a many as are in a bad way. But it's well for me as I can't go to church any longer, for if the old singers are to be done away with, there'll be nothing left as it was in Mr. Patten's time; and what's more, I hear you've settled to pull the church down and build it up new?" (Chapter I.)

This passage is a good example of the way in which George Eliot combines entertainment with the more serious business of projecting the background against which the drama of "Amos Barton" is played. She might, through objective narration, have told us that the people of Shepperton parish are conservative and have no pleasure in change, that their approach to religion is homely and pragmatic, that Amos antagonizes his parishioners by talking to them needlessly and tactlessly of sin and salvation, and that he has thrown the parish into a state of confusion by advocating the Low Church practice of hymn-singing on the one hand and the High Church practice of church restoration on the other. All this and more comes through in Mrs. Patten's words. But in addition to the information conveyed, Mrs. Patten's character is further developed and our understanding of the provincial mind is deepened. Equally important, the passage demonstrates George Eliot's perfect ear for the authentic accents of the country idiom, as indeed the characters of "Amos Barton" do whenever they open their mouths. One would say that "Amos Barton" in this respect was valuable practice for *Adam Bede,* except that the naturalness of the speech in her first story shows that George Eliot needed no practice.

In this speech of Mrs. Patten's as throughout this part of the story, George Eliot writes with affectionate irony. She invites the reader to feel an amused superiority to Mrs. Patten, but it is superiority free from any trace of contempt. The humor is no more sentimental than it is sarcastic, however. She does not deride Mrs. Patten's view of sin and salvation, but she does see through it:

> Now the fact was that the Rev. Amos Barton, on his last visit to Mrs. Patten, had urged her to enlarge her promised subscription of twenty pounds, representing to her that she was only a steward of her riches, and that she could not spend them more for the glory of God than by giving a heavy subscription towards the rebuilding of Shepperton Church— a practical precept which was not likely to smooth the way to her acceptance of his theological doctrine.

While the scene at Cross Farm is perhaps the most characteristic example of humor in "Amos Barton," it is not the only one. In the second chapter, there is a vivid and funny description of Amos' weekly visit to the Shepperton workhouse and of his efforts among the paupers there. The irony of the passage is more biting but no less amusing. Among the inmates of the workhouse are Poll Fodge, an ugly, one-eyed woman who "in spite of nature's apparent safeguards against that contingency, had contributed to the perpetuation of the Fodge characteristics in the person of a small boy, who was behaving naughtily on one of the back benches"; Mr. Fitchett, an ex-footman who "carted and uncarted manure with a sort of flunkey grace"; and Mrs. Brick, "one of those hard undying old women" to whom snuff "seemed to be an embalming powder, helping her soul to do the office of salt." It is Amos' task to "bring home the gospel to a handful of such souls," and

> to have any chance of success, short of miraculous inter-
> vention, he must bring his geographical, chronological,
> exegetical mind pretty nearly to the pauper point of view,
> or of no view; he must have some approximate conception
> of the mode in which the doctrines that have so much
> vitality in the plenum of his own brain will comport them-
> selves *in vacuo*.

Amos Barton has neither the adaptability nor the imagination to succeed on these terms:

> He talked of Israel and its sins, of chosen vessels, of the
> Paschal lamb, of blood as a medium of reconciliation; and
> he strove in this way to convey religious truth within reach
> of the Fodge and Fitchett mind. This very morning, the first
> lesson was the twelfth chapter of Exodus, and Mr. Barton's
> exposition turned on unleavened bread. Nothing in the world
> more suited to the simple understanding than instruction
> through familiar types and symbols! But there is always the
> danger attending it, that the interest or comprehension of
> your hearers may stop short precisely at the point where
> your spiritual interpretation begins. And Mr. Barton this
> morning succeeded in carrying the pauper imagination to
> the dough-tub, but unfortunately was not able to carry it
> upwards from that well-known object to the unknown
> truths which it was intended to shadow forth.

The perfect control over material shown here, the sureness of touch and the neat progression of thought, help to explain the instantaneous recognition of "Amos Barton" as the production of a fresh and original talent.

In discussing the humor of "Amos Barton" one must mention the labored facetiousness in diction and phraseology which runs through the narrator's comment, in contrast to the perfectly realistic speech of the characters. Though it strikes most modern readers as a positive defect in style, this was undoubtedly considered humorous by the first readers. A child's first learning is called "alphabetic erudition," milk in tea is "lacteal addition," thumb-sucking is an "infantine peccadillo," and blood is "circulating fluid." This ponderous Latinity does not occur only in individual phrases; the manner can be maintained at length:

> I was so crude a member of the congregation that my nurse found it necessary to provide for the reinforcement of my devotional patience by smuggling bread-and-butter into the sacred edifice. (Chapter 1.)

> The walls are smooth and innutrient as the summit of the Rev. Amos Barton's head, after ten years of baldness and supererogatory soap. (Chapter 1.)

> Right in front of him . . . sat "Old Maxum", as he was familiarly called, his real patronymic remaining a mystery to most persons. A fine philological sense discerns in this cognomen an indication that the pauper patriarch had once been considered pithy and sententious in his speech. (Chapter 2.)

Writing in this way, George Eliot was simply following a contemporary literary fashion. Victorian readers were no doubt genuinely amused when Dickens described a tip as an "appropriate pecuniary compliment" or a coat-of-arms as a "heraldic cognizance."[2] Trollope writes of Mr. Crawley's regret that his son's

---

2. *Little Dorrit* (1857), Book I, Chap. 12.

education at Mr. Arabin's expense should be "so manifestly eleemosynary,"[3] and in even the more restrained sections of *The Ordeal of Richard Feverel,* Meredith speaks of "prognostics multitudinously hinted" (meaning various guesses about Richard's future), and calls a wedding ring a "token of hymeneal devotion."[4] In "Amos Barton" this type of humor is clearly inferior to the genuine wit of George Eliot's irony, and although such instances of learned playfulness have been pointed out by critics as characteristic of the story,[5] they could not, even when they were to the current taste, have gained for "Amos Barton" its reputation for humor and fresh wit. That was soundly based upon the good-humored irony of the characterization, which like all real humor is an organic part of the work. The genius apparent in such creations as Mrs. Poyser, and Dodsons, the rustics at the Rainbow, or in the perfectly controlled irony of *Middlemarch* may be discerned already in "Amos Barton." It is not a genius that depends upon facetious pedantry and ponderous circumlocutions.

Humor—embracing as it does in "Amos Barton" character and setting—is probably the most appealing quality in the story today. It is likely that the readers of 1858 were more impressed by the pathos, and this would have pleased George Eliot, for her first aim was "to win your tears for real sorrow." She was probably fairly confident of her abilities in humorous writing—her letters reveal a natural turn for the kind of ironic characterization which appears in "Amos Barton"—but the handling of pathos was an experiment for her, and success here would have been particularly gratifying. That it was an experiment is clear in her account of Lewes' reaction to the story:

3. *The Last Chronicle of Barset* (1867), Chap. 1.
4. *The Ordeal of Richard Feverel* (1859), Chap. 4; Chap. 29.
5. See Gerald Bullett, *George Eliot, Her Life and Letters* (London, 1947), p. 163; and J. Lewis May, *George Eliot, A Study* (London, 1930), pp. 71-75.

The scene at Cross Farm, he said, satisfied him that I had the very element he had been doubtful about—it was clear that I could write good dialogue. There still remained the question whether I could command any pathos, and that was to be decided by the mode in which I treated Milly's death. One night G. went to town on purpose to leave me a quiet evening for writing it. I wrote the chapter from the news brought by the shepherd to Mrs. Hackit, to the moment when Amos is dragged from the bedside and I read it to G. when he came home. We both cried over it, and then he came up to me and kissed me, saying "I think your pathos is better than your fun."[6]

There is something of the pathetic in each of the *Scenes,* but only in "Amos Barton" is it the dominant note. The death of Milly, encompassing as it does the death of a gentle young mother and the bereavement of her husband and six children, is a classic example of the pathetic in mid-Victorian fiction, and deserves the attention of modern readers who wish to assess the taste of the Victorians in such matters. But while George Eliot was content to have her handling of pathos judged solely by the chapter dealing with Milly's death, the pathos of "Amos Barton" goes much deeper than any single scene. Were it not vitally related to the story as a whole, the pathos of Chapter 8 would be superficial— a mere patch of emotion. A consideration of George Eliot's presentation of Milly and Amos in the earlier parts of the story will show the true source of pathetic emotion in the closing chapters.

Milly Barton is one of George Eliot's most appealing creations, a woman altogether good and lovable without being improbably saintly. We first see her "softly pacing up and down by the red firelight, holding in her arms little Walter, the year-old baby, who looks over her shoulder with wide-open eyes" (Chapter 2),

6. "How I Came to Write Fiction," *Letters,* 2, 408.

and this first impression of her—"a large, fair, gentle Madonna"—
is a lasting one. Milly has no existence except as wife and mother,
but she is no painted plaster Madonna; she is unfailingly cheerful
because she is happy, but she does not sentimentalize the trials of
poverty:

> "I wish we could do without borrowing money, and yet
> I don't see how we can. Poor Fred must have some new shoes;
> I couldn't let him go to Mrs. Bond's yesterday because his
> toes were peeping out, dear child! and I can't let him walk
> anywhere except in the garden. He must have a pair before
> Sunday. Really, boots and shoes are the greatest trouble of
> my life. Everything else one can turn and turn about, and
> make old look like new; but there's no coaxing boots and
> shoes to look better than they are." (Chapter 2.)

The strength of Milly's love, as well as the essential quality of
her being, is best seen in the midst of the trials consequent upon
the Countess' extended stay at the vicarage:

> When time glided on, and the countess's visit did not end,
> Milly was not blind to any phase of their position. She knew
> of the slander; she was aware of the keeping aloof of old
> friends; but these she felt almost entirely on her husband's
> account. A loving woman's world lies within the four walls
> of her own home; and it is only through her husband that
> she is in any electric communication with the world beyond.
> Mrs. Simpkins may have looked scornfully at her but baby
> crows and holds out his little arms none the less blithely;
> Mrs. Tomkins may have left off calling on her, but her
> husband comes home none the less to receive her care and
> caresses; it has been wet and gloomy out of doors today, but
> she has looked well after the shirt buttons, has cut out baby's
> pinafores, and half-finished Willy's blouse.

So it was with Milly. She was only vexed that her husband should be vexed—only wounded because he was misconceived. (Chapter 7.)

Yet here, too, Milly is realistic. She does not sentimentally persuade herself that all will come right somehow, that God will provide, or that her love alone can overcome all trials:

> But the difficulty about ways and means she felt in quite a different manner. Her rectitude was alarmed lest they should have to make tradesmen wait for their money; her motherly love dreaded the diminution of comforts for the children; and the sense of her own failing health gave exaggerated force to these fears.

> Milly could no longer shut her eyes to the fact, that the Countess was inconsiderate, if she did not allow herself to entertain severer thoughts; and she began to feel that it would soon be a duty to tell her frankly that they really could not afford to have her visit farther prolonged. (Chapter 7.)

From the time when we first see Milly, much of the effect of the story turns upon our realization that she is the mainstay in Amos' life. The pathos of his life, as of hers, arises from the fact that she is the one bright thing in his colorless existence and he does not know it. One of the most effective elements in "Amos Barton," and an important contributing factor to the pathos of the ending, is the warmly intimate picture presented of home and hearth; our feeling about Milly gives truth to the picture and saves it from sentimentality. A few years after the publication of *Scenes of Clerical Life*, Ruskin defined the mid-Victorian concept of the home: "This is the true nature of home—it is the place of

Peace; the shelter, not only from all injury, but from all terror, doubt, and division."[7] While Ruskin can hardly be considered the most reliable authority on Victorian home-life, his words express a common attitude. It is the attitude reflected in the cosy pictures of domesticity in Dickens. One thinks of Bob Cratchit, sheltered from the cold harshness of Scrooge by the warmth of family affection, or of the Toodle family, exuding domestic bliss away from the world of Dombey and Carker. In "Amos Barton" Milly creates the shelter of the home and illuminates it with her calm, beautiful presence. "Soothing, unspeakable charm of gentle womanhood!" writes George Eliot in describing Milly (Chapter 2), and this quality in her pervades the story. Milly's significance as the soothing, sheltering influence in Amos' life may be seen in examining the sequence of description in Chapter 2, through which runs the contrast between Amos at home and Amos in the outer world—the world of injury, doubt, and division.

We first see him "returning home in the moonlight—a little chill, it is true, for he had just now no greatcoat . . . and a fur boa round one's neck, with a waterproof cape over one's shoulders, doesn't frighten away the cold from one's legs." Entering the house, he is greeted by the sight of Milly with the baby in the warm fire-lit room. The cheerful domesticity of the vicarage is further emphasized when we see the Bartons at breakfast the next morning—Milly "busy cutting bread-and-butter for five hungry mouths, while Nanny, baby on one arm, in rosy cheeks, fat neck, and nightgown, brought in a jug of hot milk-and-water." The scene is complete when we are told that "there was a blazing fire in the sitting-room, and not without need, for the vicarage garden, as they looked out on it from the bow-window, was hard with black frost, and the sky had the white woolly look that portends snow." Away from Milly and warmth of his hearth, Amos confronts a cold, unfriendly world:

7. "Of Queens' Gardens," *Sesame and Lilies* (1865), Sect. 68.

At eleven o'clock, Mr. Barton walked forth in cape and boa, with the sleet driving in his face, to read prayers at the workhouse, euphemistically called the "College"[8]. . . . A flat ugly district this; depressing enough to look at even on the brightest days. The roads are black with coal-dust, the brick houses dingy with smoke; and at that time—the time of handloom weavers—every other cottage had a loom at its window, where you might see a pale sickly-looking man or woman pressing a narrow chest against a board, and doing a sort of treadmill work with legs and arms. A troublesome district for a clergyman.

The dreary futility of Amos' labors is epitomized in his experience at the "College":

And so, while the sleet outside was turning to unquestionable snow, and the stony dining-room looked darker and drearier, and Mr. Fitchett was nodding his lowest, and Mr. Spratt was boxing the boys' ears with a constant *rinforzando,* as he felt more keenly the approach of dinner-time, Mr. Barton wound up his exhortation with something of the February chill at his heart as well as his feet.

Then we see Amos, his duties among the paupers over, returning home again, chilled and cross, to the healing warmth of Milly's love:

The snow was falling in thicker and thicker flakes, and already the vicarage-garden was cloaked in white as he passed through the gate. Mrs. Barton heard him open the door, and ran out of the sitting-room to meet him.

"I'm afraid your feet are very wet, dear. What a terrible morning! Let me take your hat. Your slippers are at the fire."

8. I have followed the manuscript reading of this sentence; all published versions of "Amos Barton" have "euphuistically" for "euphemistically" (MS fol. 28).

The sense of love and security which emanates from Milly's presence in the story gives truth to the pathos that is engendered by her loss. A comment in one of Arthur Hugh Clough's letters is pertinent here. Apropos of *Emilia Wyndham,* a novel which he considered "too pathetic a great deal," Clough wrote in 1847:

> I don't want to cry except for some good reason; it is "pleasant, but wrong" in my mind. A novel ought to make you think, and if it does that, the more vivid it is the better, and of course it follows, that now and then it will make you cry.[9]

"Amos Barton" would satisfy Clough's requirement on this point; there is a reason for the tears shed over Milly Barton's death. The reason lies in all that she is and all that she means to Amos; when we come to Milly's death, we do not question the integrity of the description.

It goes without saying that the taste for deathbed scenes has changed, if not vanished altogether, in the years since Dickens had his vast audience weeping over Little Nell. No aspect of Victorian fiction has been more harshly judged by the twentieth century than the manner in which novelists handle pathos in their books. But in our disgust at the excess of sentiment in some Victorian novels, we have perhaps been over-ready to brand as sentimental all pathos that is unmixed with irony or bitterness. The modern equivalent of the death of Paul Dombey is, as Kathleen Tillotson points out, "the long-drawn clinical horror of the death of little Phil from tubercular meningitis in Aldous Huxley's *Point Counter Point.*"[1] Or to take another example, when a little boy is killed in a hunting accident in Evelyn Waugh's *A Handful of Dust,* the height of the emotion is expressed by a groom, the boy's best friend, who says: "He'd had a lousy day too poor little bastard," and the modern reader is more moved by this than by

9. F. L. Mulhauser, ed., *Correspondence of Arthur Hugh Clough* (2 vols. Oxford, 1957), *I*, 181.
1. *Novels of the Eighteen-Forties* (Oxford, 1954), p. 50.

the death of Little Nell. In contrast to the death of Milly Barton we have the death, also in childbirth, of Catherine Barkley in *A Farewell to Arms,* whose last words are, "I'm not a bit afraid. It's just a dirty trick." The toughness with which these deaths are treated may be right for us in the historical context of the twentieth century, but to be fair to the nineteenth we can hardly deny the justice of Gissing's defense of Little Nell's death: "This pathos was true for them and for their day."[2] "His defense," says Mrs. Tillotson, "was on the right lines, the historical lines, for the response to such pathos must always be related to those changing things, manners and beliefs."[3] Under manners is included the readiness to cry which was standard equipment for most Victorian readers, men as well as women. Lord Jeffrey, whom Carlyle called "the coryphaeus of his generation,"[4] wrote concerning the death of Paul Dombey: "Oh, my dear dear Dickens! what a No. 5 you have now given us! I have so cried and sobbed over it last night, and again this morning; and felt my heart purified by those tears";[5] Albert Smith, speaking of "Amos Barton," told John Blackwood that "the death of that sweet Milly made me blubber like a boy. I did not think, at forty, I had so many tears left in me." (*Letters, 2,* 293n.) It is not simply a change in manners which prevents the modern reader's crying so easily, however; the change in belief about death is equally important. To quote Mrs. Tillotson again:

> We have also to bear in mind our other modern inhibitions, especially our inarticulateness on the subject of death (represented in 'No flowers. No letters'). The absence of a context for death in modern life, the lack of a setting of common belief—all this must impoverish its treatment in literature and the social impact of any treatment it receives.[6]

2. *The Immortal Dickens* (London, 1925), p. 199.
3. *Novels of the Eighteen-Forties,* p. 49.
4. *Reminiscences* (2 vols. London, 1881), 2, 64.
5. Lord Cockburn, *Life of Lord Jeffrey* (2 vols. Edinburgh, 1852), 2, 406.
6. *Novels of the Eighteen-Forties,* pp. 49–50.

The Victorians felt no such reticence about death, and we can have no legitimate objection to the display of their less inhibited sensibilities in their literature. But, for them as for us, a sincere sensibility degenerates into sentimentality when death is dragged into the plot of a story simply for sensation; or when we put our reactions to the fact of death above the fact itself and, losing sight of the significance of the death, concentrate solely on our feelings about it; or when the presentation of it is unnatural. Any one of these factors may result in sentimentality as generally defined—the creation or display of emotion in excess of what the occasion demands—and these are the factors to be borne in mind in considering George Eliot's treatment of the death of Milly Barton.

The first factor does not require discussion here. George Eliot is not liable to the criticism which Ruskin made of Dickens: "Nell, in *The Old Curiosity Shop,* was simply killed for the market, as a butcher kills a lamb."[7] There can be no question of Milly's death being extraneous to the plot, or of the plot's having been twisted to accommodate popular taste. The whole point of the story is to show how Milly is sacrificed to the Countess' selfishness and Amos' stupidity. As for the second factor, in the foregoing discussion I have tried to show that it is the significance of Milly's death in particular rather than a conventional feeling about death in general which is of first importance. The third point—whether the presentation of death is natural—deserves more consideration.

George Eliot makes an effective use of contrast in the description leading up to Milly's death. Chapter 7 closes on a note of calm happiness which makes the pathos that is to come more poignant:

On Sunday, after morning service, Mrs. Hackit called at the Vicarage to inquire how Mrs. Barton was, and was invited

7. "Fiction Fair and Foul," *Works of John Ruskin* (39 vols. London, 1903–12), *34,* 275n.

up-stairs to see her. Milly lay placid and lovely in her feeble-ness, and held out her hand to Mrs. Hackit with a beaming smile. It was very pleasant to her to see her old friend un-reserved and cordial once more. The seven months' baby was very tiny and very red, but "handsome is that handsome does,"—he was pronounced to be "doing well," and Mrs. Hackit went home gladdened at heart to think that the perilous hour was over.

It seems at this point that everything has after all turned out all right for the Bartons. The Countess has gone, old friends are returning, and Milly has come safely through an anxious time. Amos is still Amos and they are poorer than ever, but after the disagreeable six months just past one is content to see life at the Vicarage resume its old course. Then with the quiet unexpected-ness of real life, a change is announced:

> The following Wednesday, when Mr. and Mrs. Hackit were seated comfortably by their bright hearth, enjoying the long afternoon afforded by an early dinner, Rachel, the house-maid, came in and said,—
>
> "If you pleas'm, the shepherd says, have you heard as Mrs. Barton's wuss, and not expected to live?" (Chapter 8.)

Mrs. Hackit sets out at once for the Vicarage. The description of events following her arrival there maintains the simple, straight-forward manner in which the chapter opens. Mrs. Hackit is as unsentimental as a person can be, and her presence in the scene contributes much to the credibility of the passage. Through Mrs. Hackit, George Eliot suggests the activity of real life in the pres-ence of death. From her we get a vivid sense of the reality sur-rounding death, which is very important to the effect of the pathos, for it is the sense of reality which enables us to believe in the pathos. Aldous Huxley's comments on Dickens are illuminating in this connection:

One of Dickens' most striking peculiarities is that, whenever in his writing he becomes emotional, he ceases instantly to use his intelligence. The overflowing of his heart drowns his head and even dims his eyes; for whenever he is in the melting mood, Dickens ceases to be able and probably ceases even to wish to see reality. . . . Mentally drowned and blinded by the sticky overflowings of his heart, Dickens was incapable, when moved, of re-creating, in terms of art, the reality which had moved him, was even, it would seem, unable to perceive that reality. . . . The emotion-blinded Dickens noticed practically nothing of what went on in Little Nelly's neighbourhood during the child's last days.[8]

Whether or not this is completely true of Dickens is not the point; what is important here is that Huxley suggests one of the pitfalls into which a writer may stumble in dealing with the pathetic. George Eliot avoids it. With perfectly controlled emotion, she gives a realistic picture of what was going on while Milly lay dying. Nothing could be less melodramatic than Mrs. Hackit's arrival at the Vicarage and her exchange with Nanny, the Bartons' nurse and cook:

It was a bright frosty day, and by the time Mrs. Hackit arrived at the Vicarage, the sun was near its setting. There was a carriage and pair standing at the gate, which she recognized as Dr. Madeley's, the physician from Rotherby. She entered at the kitchen door that she might avoid knocking, and quietly question Nanny. No one was in the kitchen, but, passing on, she saw the sitting-room door open, and Nanny, with Walter in her arms, removing the knives and forks, which had been laid for dinner three hours ago.

"Master says he can't eat no dinner," was Nanny's first word. "He's never tasted nothin' sin' yesterday mornin', but a cup o' tea."

8. *Vulgarity in Literature* (London, 1930), pp. 56–57.

"When was your missis took worse?"

"O' Monday night. They sent for Dr. Madeley i' the middle o' the day yesterday, an' he's here again now."

"Is the baby alive?"

"No, it died last night. The children's all at Mrs. Bond's. She come and took 'em away last night, but the master says they must be fetched soon. He's up-stairs now, wi' Dr. Madeley and Mr. Brand." (Chapter 8.)

The simple realism of this scene conveys an immediate sense of the presence of death in the house. While Mrs. Hackit and Nanny are talking, Amos comes in "with dry despairing eyes, haggard and unshaven," and when he sees Mrs. Hackit move towards him "with answering sorrow in her face," he breaks down. Mrs. Hackit's words of comfort to him show an instinctive tact in avoiding cant or triteness. She says just what would probably be said in actual life: " 'Bear up, Mr. Barton,' Mrs. Hackit ventured to say at last, 'bear up, for the sake o' them dear children.' " This recalls Amos to himself and to Milly's wish to see the children.

It is in the matter of the children that some modern readers find fault with the pathos of "Amos Barton." Joan Bennett, to take for example the critic who has been most severe on this point, writes: "It is all too easy to draw tears by describing the death of a devoted mother who summons her children one by one to her bedside and harrows their feelings with her 'selfless' dying words"; Mrs. Bennett adds that upon reflection the pathos does not ring true.[9] But such scenes were undoubtedly acted out in thousands of Victorian homes as a parent lay dying—at Windsor in 1861, to give a well-known instance—and nineteenth-century memoirs abound in such descriptions as this by Emily Eden of her sister Mary's death in 1862:

I am most thankful I was able to witness such a really happy deathbed as hers, so calm, so peaceful, and her mind as en-

9. *George Eliot, Her Mind and Her Art* (Cambridge, 1948), p. 92.

tirely clear as it ever was in its best days. And to see those six tall sons, four daughters-in-law, and her three daughters all round her bed, the sons more overwhelmed even than the daughters, and she thanking them, and saying how happy they had made her, it was a scene that quite comforts me for her loss, and her poor daughters had quite the same feeling.[1]

Milly's deathbed reflects the experience of real life, and should not be aspersed as mere sentimental conventionality.

The scene between Milly and the children is dealt with in the space of less than one page, and though upon analyzing it we may feel that certain adjectives ("poor," "little," "sweet") are overworked, the effect in reading is of swift simplicity. It is hardly fair to say that Milly harrows the children's feelings with her selfless words. Her dying admonition, if conventional, is perfectly simple: "Patty will try to be your mamma when I am gone, my darlings. You will be good, and not vex her." George Eliot does not exploit the pathos to anything like the degree permitted by the standards of the day. And she keeps a firm grasp on reality, noting that the children cried "because mamma was ill and papa looked so unhappy; but they thought, perhaps next week things would be as they used to be again." The same sense of reality illuminates the description of Dickey Barton at his mother's funeral, looking first up at the minister then "down at the coffin, and thinking he and Chubby would play at that when they got home."

John Blackwood objected to the particularization of the children at the deathbed, not because he felt it an unnatural lingering over the sad scene, but because "the reader had not been prepared to care for them individually but simply as a group." (*Letters, 2,* 283.) George Eliot replied: "I think the particularization of the children in the deathbed scene has an important effect on the imagination." (*Letters, 2,* 288.) Clearly she thought of the chil-

---

1. Violet Dickinson, ed., *Miss Eden's Letters* (London, 1919), p. 403.

dren not as mere pathetic accessories, but as significant figures in a meaningful pattern of pathos. In another instance, where the children did *not* make a meaningful contribution to the action, she bowed to Blackwood's judgment. He had objected also to the particularization of the young Bartons in the Conclusion, and George Eliot altered this part of the story accordingly. The manuscript reads: "All the other children were now grown up, and had gone their separate ways. Sophy and Chubby were married. Fred was a banker's clerk and already a family man. Walter had gone to sea and Dickey, you will be glad to hear, had shown remarkable talents as an engineer." (MS fol. 110.) In publication, the second and third sentences and the first six words of the last were omitted. The reference to Dickey was retained because he had previously been more individualized than the others.

Once the children are gone from Milly's deathbed the scene is brought quickly to a close:

> Milly kept her eyes shut for some time after the children were gone. Amos had sunk on his knees, and was holding her hand while he watched her face. By-and-by she opened her eyes, and, drawing him close to her, whispered slowly,—
>
> "My dear—dear—husband—you have been—very—good to me. You—have—made me—very—happy."
>
> She spoke no more for many hours. They watched her breathing becoming more and more difficult, until evening deepened into night, and until midnight was past. About half-past twelve she seemed to be trying to speak, and they leaned to catch her words.
>
> "Music—music—didn't you hear it?"
>
> Amos knelt by the bed and held her hand in his. He did not believe in his sorrow. It was a bad dream. He did not know when she was gone.

As a mid-Victorian deathbed scene, this description is remarkable for what it leaves out. Milly's last rational words to Amos contrast sharply with the kind of deathbed moralizing commonly associated with Victorian fiction. Mrs. Gaskell for instance, not a particularly sentimental writer and one whom George Eliot admired, uses the deathbed for this purpose in *Sylvia's Lovers* (1863). The heroine reproaches herself (as Amos Barton might have been made to reproach himself) with having been unkind to Philip, her dying husband, but he offers reassurance:

> "No!" said Philip, turning his face, forgetful of himself in his desire to comfort her. "God pities us as a father pities his poor wandering children; the nearer I come to death the clearer I see Him. But you and me have done wrong to each other; yet we can see now how we were led to it; we can pity and forgive one another. I'm getting low and faint, lassie; but thou must remember this; God knows more, and is more forgiving than either you to me, or me to you. I think and do believe as we shall meet together before His face." (Chapter 45.)

The colloquial turn of this speech makes it more readily believable, more moving perhaps, than it otherwise would be, but one still feels that the words are Mrs. Gaskell's more than Philip's. If the speech cannot be called sentimental, it is nonetheless artificial, and the artificiality invests the description of Philip's death with a certain insincerity. Pure sentimentalism is more apparent in a subsequent passage in the same chapter:

> It seemed but yesterday since he was a little boy at his mother's knee, wishing with all the earnestness of his childish heart to be like Abraham, who was called the friend of God, or David, who was said to be the man after God's own heart, or St. John, who was called "the Beloved." As very present seemed the day on which he made resolutions of trying to be like them; it was in the spring, and some one had brought in cowslips; and the scent of those flowers was in his nostrils

now, as he lay a-dying—his life ended, his battles fought, his time for "being good" over and gone—the opportunity, once given in all eternity, past.

The pathos here is self-conscious, the contrast between childish innocence and mature sorrow too obvious. It is a contrast often made in Victorian deathbed literature, however. One of the best known instances is the death of Colonel Newcome:

> At the usual evening hour the chapel bell began to toll, and Thomas Newcome's hands outside the bed feebly beat time. And just as the last bell struck, a peculiar sweet smile shone over his face, and he lifted up his head a little, and quickly said "Ad sum!" and fell back. It was the word we used at school, when names were called; and lo, he, whose heart was as that of a little child, had answered to his name, and stood in the presence of the Master.[2]

And there are the dying words of old Alice in *Mary Barton* who "imagined herself once again in the happy, happy realms of childhood": " 'Mother, good night! Dear mother! bless me once more! I'm very tired, and would fain go to sleep.' She never spoke again this side heaven."[3]

Milly's hallucination at the last is certainly conventional,[4] but the handling of it is notably restrained in comparison with most mid-Victorian treatments of the deathbed "miracle." A characteris-

2. *The Newcomes,* Chap. 80.
3. Chap. 33.
4. Walter E. Houghton thinks the convention reflects a "desire to make the deathbed serve the cause of antiskepticism," that the mention of heavenly music or reunion with loved ones was "sufficient to invoke a powerful sense of reassurance." (*The Victorian Frame of Mind, 1830–1870* [New Haven, 1957], p. 277 and note.) Besides Milly's, Mr. Houghton refers in this connection to the deaths of Little Nell in *The Old Curiosity Shop* (1841), Chap. 71; Margaret in Miss Yonge's *The Daisy Chain* (1856), Part II, Chap. 25; and Muriel in Mrs. Craik's *John Halifax, Gentleman* (1857), Chap. 28.

tic example occurs in a story called "Hester Benfield" published in *Blackwood's* the month after this part of "Amos Barton" appeared. Here is the heroine's departure from earth:

> Her peace was made with all, and in the sombre twilight, with the gentle loving heart of old restored to her, Hester was passing away. "Hark! did you not hear a voice calling me? It is my Mary's. I see her now; she is going to bear me upwards on her bosom. Dearest husband, I may not stay— kiss me, and let me depart. Frank, my dear dutiful son, forgive me; let me clasp you once more," and in that close embrace her last sigh was breathed.[5]

This is typical of the theatricality, the self-consciousness that destroys any sense of sincerity, which George Eliot avoids in describing the death of Milly. She does not have Milly die with one eye on Heaven and the other on her audience. Nor does she attempt to wring the reader's heart more that it will be wrung by the simple facts of the situation. Contrast, for instance, Dickens' treatment of Little Nell's death:

> For she was dead. There, upon her little bed, she lay at rest. The solemn stillness was no marvel now.
>
> She was dead. No sleep so beautiful and calm, so free from trace of pain, so fair to look upon. She seemed a creature fresh from the hand of God, and waiting for the breath of life; not one who had lived and suffered death.
>
> Her couch was dressed with here and there some winter berries and green leaves, gathered in a spot she had been used to favour. "When I die, put near me something that has loved the light, and had the sky above it always." Those were her words. She was dead. Dear, gentle, patient, noble Nell was dead. Her little bird—a poor slight thing the pressure of a finger would have crushed—was stirring nimbly

5. *Blackwood's Edinburgh Magazine*, *81* (March 1857), p. 354.

in its cage; and the strong heart of its child-mistress was mute and motionless for ever.[6]

When Milly dies—and it is worth remarking that death comes so quietly that Amos is unaware of it—the scene is over. The pathos is there and George Eliot does not feel it necessary to slip into alliterative blank verse and moralize as Dickens does when Nell dies:

When Death strikes down the innocent and young, for every fragile form from which he lets the panting spirit free, a hundred virtues rise, in shapes of mercy, charity, and love, to walk the world, and bless it. Of every tear that sorrowing mortals shed on such green graves, some good is born, some gentler nature comes. In the Destroyer's steps there spring up bright creations that defy his power, and his dark path becomes a way of light to Heaven.[7]

The following passage may be set beside the description of the Vicarage in Chapter 2 as showing the change which Milly's death makes in Amos' life. The poignancy of this description depends upon our recollection of the earlier scenes:

The burial was over, and Amos turned with his children to re-enter the house—the house where, an hour ago, Milly's dear body lay, where the windows were half-darkened, and sorrow seemed to have a hallowed precinct for itself, shut out from the world. But now she was gone; the broad snow-reflected daylight was in all the rooms; the Vicarage again seemed part of the common working-day world, and Amos, for the first time, felt that he was alone—that day after day, month after month, year after year, would have to be lived through without Milly's love. Spring would come, and she would not be there; summer, and she would not be there; and

6. *The Old Curiosity Shop,* Chap. 71.
7. Ibid., Chap. 72.

he would never have her again with him by the fireside in the long evenings. (Chapter 9.)

The pathos here escapes sentimentality because the sentiment has been so fully prepared for in the depiction of Milly's character; she has been brought warmly alive for us and we feel a real sense of loss at her death. We see, thinking back over the story, that we are being asked to cry for "some good reason." Nothing could give a more poignant sense of Amos' loss than the simple statement: "The broad snow-reflected daylight was in all the rooms."[8] The words suggest the emptiness, the coldness, the steely greyness of Amos' future, while recalling by contrast the warmth that filled the house when Milly was there, and we share Amos' sense of desolation. The effect is created with no lapse of taste: we are shown no half-finished little stocking, no empty chair by the fireside, no cradle now forever still.

The pathos of "Amos Barton" is genuine, for it derives from the circumstances of the story and is not a superimposed effect. Milly's death is a meaningful and necessary element in the structure of the whole: we can believe in Amos' suffering and in the sympathy it arouses among his parishioners because we can believe in the beauty of Milly's life and the sadness of her death. Moreover, the pathos is treated in a simple, natural way which precludes at once both falsity and sentimentality. George Eliot's art, as well as her taste, is the more remarkable for avoiding the exaggerated style acceptable at the time. With the single exception of the description in Chapter 10 of Amos' last visit to Milly's grave before leaving Shepperton ("Gradually, as his eye dwelt on the words, 'Amelia, the beloved wife,' the waves of feeling swelled

8. Barbara Hardy has noted in George Eliot's work the recurring image of "the disenchanted day-lit room." See "The Moment of Disenchantment in George Eliot's Novels," *Review of English Studies,* N. S. 5 (1954), 256–64. Miss Hardy finds the first instance of it in "Janet's Repentance," Chap. 16, but this passage from "Amos Barton" seems equally to the point.

within his soul, and he threw himself on the grave, clasping it with his arms, and kissing the cold turf."), the pathos of "Amos Barton" is as natural as the humor. One has no difficulty in believing that John Blackwood was sincere when he told George Eliot: "It is a long time since I have read anything so fresh so humorous and so touching." (*Letters, 2, 283.*)

"MR. GILFIL'S LOVE STORY": ROMANCE AND MELODRAMA

The first chapter of "Mr. Gilfil's Love Story," in its easy, natural style and in the charm of its descriptions, more than fulfills the promise of "Amos Barton." The second "scene," like the first, opens on a note of reminiscence:

> When old Mr. Gilfil died, thirty years ago, there was general sorrow in Shepperton; and if black cloth had not been hung round the pulpit and reading-desk, by order of his nephew and principal legatee, the parishioners would certainly have subscribed the necessary sum out of their own pockets, rather than allow such a tribute of respect to be wanting.

In a brief look at provincial mourning habits George Eliot displays the kind of humor, managed with the ease of intimate knowledge, which will reappear in the presentation of the Dodson sisters in *The Mill on the Floss*. All the farmers' wives, we are told, "brought out their best black bombasines":

> An unreadiness to put on black on all available occasions, or too great an alacrity in putting it off, argued, in Mrs. Higgins's opinion, a dangerous levity of Character, and an unnatural insensibility to the essential fitness of things.
>
> "Some folks can't a-bear to put off their colours," she remarked; "but that was never the way i' *my* family. Why, Mrs. Parrot, from the time I was married, till Mr. Higgins

died, nine year ago come Candlemas, I niver was out o' black two year together!"

"Ah," said Mrs. Parrot, who was conscious of inferiority in this respect, "there isn't many families as have had so many deaths as yours, Mrs. Higgins."

Mrs. Higgins and Mrs. Parrot appear before us without the slightest trace of self-consciousness, either on their part or on George Eliot's; in this small illumination of their lives we seem at once to gain a personal familiarity with the whole society in which they move. Perhaps the chief charm of the *Scenes of Clerical Life* lies in the intimate sense of Shepperton which is created, the sense of a place where things change but slowly and where life is conducted according to long-established custom and prejudice. One is aware of this background throughout "Amos Barton," but it is nowhere more charmingly presented than in the first chapter of "Mr. Gilfil's Love Story." It is the highest tribute to the art of such writing to say that it seems completely natural.

Toward the end of the chapter we renew acquaintance with Mrs. Patten and Mr. Hackit; as in "Amos Barton," they are discussing their pastor, and their talk contributes to the sense of background here as it did in the earlier story. We are told that Mr. Hackit,

who had not come into the parish until ten years after Mrs. Gilfil's death, would often put old questions to Mrs. Patten for the sake of getting the old answers, which pleased him in the same way as passages from a favourite book, or the scenes of a familiar play, please more accomplished people;[9]

and as we hear Mr. Hackit asking the old questions and getting the old answers, we become aware of the pleasure of talk in rural

9. Following the phrase "more accomplished people," the words "like you, dear reader" have been deleted from the MS. (Fol. 18.)

communities, where time is a leisurely unfolding of events, and where the advent of a delicate, foreign-looking bride is still a matter of interest forty years after the fact. Mr. Hackit's conversation with Mrs. Patten must be read in full to be appreciated, but even in excerpts one observes the sureness of touch and the perfect ear for country idiom which mark George Eliot's best work in the *Scenes:*

"Ah, you remember well the Sunday as Mrs. Gilfil first come to church, eh, Mrs. Patten?"

"To be sure I do. It was a fine bright Sunday as ever was seen, just at the beginnin' o' hay harvest. Mr. Tarbett preached that day, and Mr. Gilfil sat i' the pew wi' his wife. I think I see him now, a-leadin' her up th' aisle, an' her head not reachin' much above his elber: a little pale woman, wi' eyes as black as sloes, an' yet lookin' blank-like, as if she see'd nothin' wi' em."

"I warrant she had her weddin' clothes on?" said Mr. Hackit.

"Nothin' partickler smart—on'y a white hat tied down under her chin, an' a white Indy muslin gown. But you don't know what Mr. Gilfil was in those times. He was fine an' altered afore you come into the parish. He'd a fresh colour then, an' a bright look wi' his eyes, as did your heart good to see. He looked rare an' happy that Sunday, but somehow, I'd a feelin' as it wouldn't last long. I've no opinion o' furriners, Mr. Hackit, for I've travelled i' their country wi' my lady in my time, an' seen anuff o' their victuals an' their nasty ways."

"Mrs. Gilfil came from It'ly, didn't she?"

"I reckon she did, but I niver could rightly hear about that. Mr. Gilfil was niver to be spoke to about her, and nobody else hereabout knowed anythin'. Howiver, she must ha' come over pretty young, for she spoke English as well

124

as you an' me. It's them Italians as has such fine voices, an'
Mrs. Gilfil sung, you never heared the like."

Throughout the opening chapter of "Mr. Gilfil's Love Story"
George Eliot maintains the simple manner of "Amos Barton."
The rest of the second "scene," however, is very different from
the first. "Amos Barton" is a story of quiet humor and tender
pathos; "Mr. Gilfil's Love Story," between the introductory chapter and the epilogue, is all romance and melodrama.

A romance requires a romantic setting and for this George
Eliot drew on her memories of Arbury Hall, as she had drawn on
her memories of Chilvers Coton for "Amos Barton." But there is
a difference. When she turns from the simple Shepperton background which was so intimately a part of her own experience to
the aristocratic setting of Cheverel Manor which she knew only
as an outsider, she is noticeably less sure of her descriptive power.
The sense of Shepperton grows naturally from the talk of the
people, from constant but unobtrusive references to weather and
seasons, and from passing glances at fields and farm-houses, dusty
country roads and cheerful firesides; there is very little that can
be called formal scene-setting. Cheverel Manor, on the other hand,
requires painstakingly detailed description, in which one is wearied
with the seemingly endless process of adding phrase on phrase.
The following passage is characteristic:

A charming picture Cheverel Manor would have made that
evening, if some English Watteau had been there to paint it:
the castellated house of grey-tinted stone, with the flickering
sunbeams sending dashes of golden light across the many-
shaped panes in the mullioned windows, and a great beech
leaning athwart one of the flanking towers, and breaking,
with its dark flattened boughs, the too formal symmetry of
the front; the broad gravel-walk winding on the right, by a
row of tall pines, alongside the pool—on the left branching
out among swelling grassy mounds, surmounted by clumps

of trees, where the red trunk of the Scotch fir glows in the descending sunlight against the bright green of limes and acacias; the great pool, where a pair of swans are swimming lazily with one leg tucked under a wing, and where the open water-lilies lie calmly accepting the kisses of fluttering light-sparkles; the lawn, with its smooth emerald greenness, sloping down to the rougher and browner herbage of the park, from which it is invisibly fenced by a little stream that winds away from the pool, and disappears under a wooden bridge in the distant pleasure-ground. (Chapter 2.)

The description of the interior is no better. Here is the Gothicized dining-room:

A piece of matting stretched from door to door, a bit of worn carpet under the dining-table, and a side-board in a deep recess, did not detain the eye for a moment from the lofty groined ceiling, with its richly-carved pendants, all of creamy white, relieved here and there by touches of gold. On one side, this lofty ceiling was supported by pillars and arches, beyond which a lower ceiling, a miniature copy of the higher one, covered the square projection which, with its three large pointed windows, formed the central feature of the building. (Chapter 2.)

The awkwardness of the writing here is probably due to George Eliot's desire to be absolutely faithful to what must have been one of the most impressive of remembered childhood scenes, Arbury Hall. But in keeping her eyes so firmly fixed on her model, she allows her imagination little play, and the picture is at best merely conventional and at worst tedious. In the last quoted sentences there is an effort of crowding arising from the attempt to get in all the detail, and the final sentence of the paragraph does nothing to mitigate the clumsiness of style:

The room looked less like a place to dine in than a piece of space enclosed simply for the sake of beautiful outline; and the small dining-table, with the party round it, seemed an odd and insignificant accident, rather than anything connected with the original purpose of the apartment.

The rest of the description of Cheverel Manor is equally overloaded with detail, set forth in prepositional phrases strung out in series. This sentence is characteristic:

But finding the cushions deserted, he walked on to the eastern front of the building, where, by the side of the grand entrance, was the large bow-window of the saloon, opening on to the gravel-sweep, and looking towards a long vista of undulating turf, bordered by tall trees, which, seeming to unite itself with the green of the meadows and a grassy road through a plantation, only terminated with the Gothic arch of a gateway in the far distance. (Chapter 2.)

The careful accuracy of the description of Cheverel Manor makes little impression on the imagination, and all the verbiage expended upon it cannot make the place seem real in the way that Cross Farm is real. It remains a painted backdrop, the flat, crowded surface of which reminds one of certain Pre-Raphaelite paintings, which share with this description the mid-nineteenth-century predilection for meticulously detailed representation.

George Eliot's lack of intimate familiarity with her material is also reflected in the treatment of characters. Sir Christopher and Lady Cheverel, Miss Assher and Captain Wybrow are as different from Mrs. Patten and the Hackits as Cheverel Manor is different from Cross Farm. The farm folk of Shepperton are real to us because they were real to George Eliot; the aristocrats, not being people with whom their creator had any vital connection, seem stagey and artificial. Their literary quality was pointed out by a contemporary critic: "Sir Christopher and Lady Cheverel strike us as old acquaintances whom we have known not in real life, but in books."[1] The first description of Lady Cheverel shows the conventionality of George Eliot's conception:

> She is nearly fifty, but her complexion is still fresh and beautiful, with the beauty of an auburn blond; her proud pouting lips, and her head thrown a little backward as she walks, give an expression of hauteur which is not contradicted by the cold grey eye. The tucked-in kerchief, rising full over the low tight boddice of her blue dress, sets off the majestic form of her bust, and she treads the lawn as if she were one of Sir Joshua Reynolds's stately ladies, who had suddenly stepped from her frame to enjoy the evening cool. (Chapter 2.)

The proud mouth, the head thrown back, the cold eye, and the majestic form are the usual equipment of ladies who are described as stately, a word used again and again in reference to Lady Cheverel. Sir Christopher is described in terms equally conventional: "as fine a specimen of the old English gentleman as could well have been found," with an "aquiline" nose and "penetrating" eyes. (Chapter 2.) There is nothing in the characterization of either to set them apart from the types which they represent—the "splendid old gentleman" and the "stately lady."

Another conventional type is the "highborn beauty" (so described in Chapter 2) Miss Assher, Wybrow's fiancée. Though better done, she is of the same literary genus as Charlotte Brontë's Blanche Ingram. Physically, the two ladies might be sisters:

> Miss Assher was tall, and gracefully though substantially formed, carrying herself with an air of mingled graciousness and self-confidence; her dark brown hair, untouched by

---

1. *Quarterly Review, 108* (October 1860), 478. This statement is more just than most of those made in this hostile review of George Eliot's first three books.

powder, hanging in bushy curls round her face, and falling behind in long thick ringlets nearly to her waist. (Chapter 5.)

Miss Ingram is "moulded like a Dian"; particular attention is given to "the noble bust, the sloping shoulders, the graceful neck, the dark eyes and black ringlets." She is said to be "remarkably self-conscious indeed."[2] Like Miss Ingram, Miss Assher is accompanied by a doting mother. In both stories, of course, the handsome aristocratic lady serves mainly to throw the humble heroine into eclipse. It is interesting, however, to note the differences between George Eliot's and Charlotte Brontë's treatment of so similar a situation. If Miss Assher is a stock figure of romantic fiction, she nevertheless escapes the utter unreality which makes it impossible to take Blanche Ingram seriously. Miss Assher's condescension to Caterina is portrayed with a good deal more subtlety than is found in Blanche's crude remarks about governesses, and her confusion and resentment at the situation between Wybrow and Caterina are to some extent believable. She occasionally speaks lines worthy of the worst Victorian magazine fiction, as when she tells Wybrow, "I decline any share in the affection of a man who forfeits my respect by duplicity" (Chapter 8), but she herself is not laughable, as Blanche is when addressing her mother as "Baroness Ingram of Ingram Park" and "my lady mother," or when telling Rochester: "Here then is a Corsair song. Know that I dote on Corsairs; and for that reason, sing it 'con spirito.' "[3]

It should be noted that in presenting the highborn visitors to Cheverel Manor, George Eliot is alive to the comic possibilities of the situation. We see Lady Cheverel "serenely radiant in the assurance a single glance had given her of Lady Assher's inferiority" (Chapter 5), and Lady Assher herself, foolish and talkative but

2. *Jane Eyre,* Chap. 17.
3. Ibid.

rather likable, is a pleasant surprise, running on incessantly about servants and sickness, or detailing the virtues of the late Sir John to whoever will listen:

> When the ladies were in the drawing-room again, Lady Assher was soon deep in a statement to Lady Cheverel of her views about burying people in woollen.
>
> "To be sure, you must have a woollen dress, because it's the law, you know; but that need hinder no one from putting linen underneath. I always used to say, 'If Sir John died to-morrow, I would bury him in his shirt;' and I did. And let me advise you to do so by Sir Christopher. You never saw Sir John, Lady Cheverel. He was a large tall man, with a nose just like Beatrice, and so very particular about his shirts."
> (Chapter 5.)

Here George Eliot shows considerable skill in the difficult business of presenting a bore without being boring; one is again reminded of Jane Austen—of Miss Bates in *Emma,* or of Mr. Collins in *Pride and Prejudice.* The individualizing of Lady Assher, however, in itself another indication of the originality of the new author, only serves to emphasize the conventionality of the other characters.

Captain Wybrow is interesting as George Eliot's first attempt to portray a young man of romantic appeal. Arthur Donnithorne in *Adam Bede* and Stephen Guest in *The Mill on the Floss* are both related to him, though in different ways. Dickens' comment on Wybrow is significant: "The selfish young fellow with the heart disease, in 'Mr. Gilfil's Love-Story,' is plainly taken from a woman's point of view."[4] In this Wybrow is also related to Will Ladislaw in *Middlemarch* and Daniel Deronda. The following description will show the justice of Dickens' observation; in face and figure, it will be noted, Wybrow is as conventional as Sir

4. Letter to John Blackwood, January 27, 1858. *Letters, 2,* 427.

Christopher and Lady Cheverel, being the typical aristocratic
lover of romantic fiction.

> If this young man had been less elegant in his person, he
> would have been remarked for the elegance of his dress. But
> the perfections of his slim well-proportioned figure were so
> striking that no one but a tailor could notice the perfections
> of his velvet coat; and his small white hands, with their blue
> veins and taper fingers, quite eclipsed the beauty of his lace
> ruffles. . . . Nothing could be more delicate than the blond
> complexion—its bloom set off by the powdered hair—than
> the veined overhanging eyelids, which gave an indolent ex-
> pression to the hazel eyes; nothing more finely cut than the
> transparent nostril and the short upper-lip. (Chapter 2.)

Wybrow is even more romantic for having a weak heart. The
effect of his presence on Caterina is also presented in conventionally romantic terms, of interest only as foreshadowing the glamor
of Stephen Guest: "Suddenly a breath of warmth and roses seemed
to float towards her, and an arm stole gently round her waist,
while a soft hand took up her tiny fingers. Caterina felt an electric
thrill." (Chapter 2.) And again: "But when she heard him come
in, and the scent of roses floated towards her, her heart gave one
great leap. She knew nothing till he was pressing her hand."
(Chapter 5.)

Of the young men to whom George Eliot's heroines lose their
hearts, it is Arthur Donnithorne who most closely resembles
Wybrow. In the following passage, one recognizes something
of the method as well as the material which will go into the creation of Hetty Sorrel's seducer:

> There was little company kept at the Manor, and Captain
> Wybrow would have been much duller if Caterina had not
> been there. It was pleasant to pay her attentions—to speak

to her in gentle tones, to see her little flutter of pleasure, the blush that just lit up her pale cheek, and the momentary timid glance of her dark eyes, when he praised her singing. ... What idle man can withstand the temptation of a woman to fascinate ... especially when it is quite clear to himself that he means no mischief, and shall leave everything to come right again by-and-by. At the end of eighteen months, however, during which Captain Wybrow had spent much of his time at the Manor, he found that matters had reached a point which he had not at all contemplated. Gentle tones had led to tender words, and tender words had called forth a response of looks which made it impossible not to carry on the *crescendo* of love-making. To find oneself adored by a little, graceful, dark-eyed, sweet-singing woman, whom no one need despise, is an agreeable sensation ... and also imposes some return of tenderness as a duty. (Chapter 4.)

One might almost consider Wybrow a rough sketch for Arthur if he had any of Arthur's good qualities—his real tenderness and truly affectionate nature, for instance, or his conscience. Wybrow and Arthur are alike in their selfishness and in the lightness with which they tamper with a young girl's affections. In both cases, George Eliot goes behind the trifling to show how an idle flirtation may develop into a serious, even tragic, situation. The minute investigation of personality and the careful exposition of motive and self-delusion which we find in *Adam Bede* are only faintly suggested in the treatment of Wybrow, but the paragraph which follows the one quoted above contains several indications of the psychological insight brought so brilliantly into play in the presentation of Arthur Donnithorne. We are told that Anthony "was rarely led into any conduct of which he could not give a plausible account of himself," and we think of Arthur's complicated attempts to justify his feelings to himself; we are told that nature had given Anthony "a large amount of serene self-satisfaction" and we recall Arthur's pleasure in the picture he presents to the world; we are told that "Captain Wybrow always did the thing easiest and most agreeable to him from a sense of duty," and we remember Mr. Irwine's gently ironic view of Arthur's benevolence.

"Mr. Gilfil's Love Story" is not *Adam Bede,* however, and Anthony Wybrow is no Arthur Donnithorne. While the similarity between the two is interesting (and one can hardly help thinking that the creation of Anthony was a valuable and perhaps necessary prelude to the creation of Arthur) the difference between them is of more significance, for in observing this difference one sees the amazingly swift development of George Eliot's powers in creating and portraying character. The very crudeness and conventionality of Wybrow throw into relief the fine artistry of Arthur Donnithorne's presentation. Arthur is a young man with whom it is easy to sympathize because of the truth with which his weaknesses are revealed; the attractive side of his character is, as in real life, so inextricable a part of his failings that it is impossible not to believe in him and pity him. There is no such subtlety in the presentation of Wybrow; we are warned at the outset not to believe in his charm. In the description of him quoted above one sentence was omitted which must be noted now: "The face, however—it was difficult to say why—was certainly not pleasing." The first time we see Wybrow and Caterina alone, we find him thinking: "Poor little Tina! it would make her very happy to have me." (Chapter 2.) We can hardly believe in him after this, and are not surprised later when he thinks to himself: "Heigho! Those are lucky fellows that have no women falling in love with them." (Chapter 10.) Instead of character analysis or dramatic presentation of personality, we are thus crudely given thoughts intended to be revealing, and though there is much in Wybrow that is interesting in the light of George Eliot's later achievement, he fails to be either interesting or believable as a character in his own right.

The presentation of Caterina deserves a rather more detailed examination than has been given the other characters discussed here. Caterina, as George Eliot's first attempt to portray a girl in love, is, like Wybrow, a piece of apprentice work. The experience gained in telling Caterina's story was undoubtedly valuable practice for the creation of Hetty Sorrel and Maggie Tulliver, two other victims of infatuation. Caterina, like Hetty, is hopelessly in love with a man whose social position makes marriage impossible; in both cases the love is kept secret. Each girl is the victim of a careless flirtation, and each eventually agrees to marry the faithful suitor whom family and friends had all along considered a good match. The connection between Caterina and Maggie is less obvious, consisting mainly of a similarity in suggesting the overmastering physical attraction against which each girl struggles.

In some ways, Caterina is the least satisfactory character in "Mr. Gilfil's Love Story." Though it is essential to the effect of the whole that one sympathize with her, it is difficult to do more than pity her. Even this is not easy, for it is hard ever to believe in Caterina as a person or in the fierceness of her passion for Wybrow. The first obstacle to credibility is the overly romantic way in which she is described. The "fairy tread," the "large dark eyes," and the "absence of bloom on her young cheek," all mentioned at her first appearance (Chapter 2), are recognizable attributes of the romantic heroine. The comparison of Caterina to a gypsy changeling at the end of Chapter 2 does not make her more original or individual. In Chapter 3, the romantic mist thickens as we learn of her background: she is the daughter of a penniless Milanese singer, who, on his deathbed, sends for Lady Cheverel to entreat her care for his infant. The foreign background seems thrown in simply for glamor and romance. Caterina calls Sir Christopher "padroncello" (an improbable touch, since she was brought to England when she was two years old), but any specifically Italian quality in her nature is lacking in the characterization unless we accept petulance towards Anthony and rudeness to Miss Assher as signs of Latin temperament. The anguish of her thwarted love is not in itself convincingly drawn, and one resists making the stock response to the suggestion of southern passion.

There is no complexity to Caterina's character and very little depth. We are not able to see her as a feeling, suffering human being because the description of her suffering is given in terms so explicit as to render unnecessary any imaginative response on the part of the reader. We are told at the outset that her heart was "rather sad," so we are spared the trouble of finding it out for ourselves, and the author is spared the trouble of showing it in any subtle way. The following passage demonstrates the way in which George Eliot may be said to take a short-cut around the dramatic development of her story:

> There was a voice speaking in Caterina's mind to which she had never yet given vent. That voice said continually, "Why did he make me love him—why did he let me know he loved me, if he knew all the while that he couldn't brave everything for my sake?" Then love answered, "He was led on by the feeling of the moment, as you have been, Caterina; and now you ought to help him to do what is right." Then the voice rejoined, "It was a slight matter to him. He doesn't much mind giving you up. He will soon love that beautiful woman, and forget a poor little pale thing like you." (Chapter 2.)

The method here is, to be sure, dictated to some extent by the form, the short story not permitting the more subtle and detailed treatment expected in a novel. Even so, one feels that it should not be necessary to spell out the heroine's emotional conflict in such elementary terms. This rather superficial exposition of Caterina's feelings is finished off tidily with the comment, "Thus love, anger, and jealousy were struggling in that young soul." One is not disposed to accept so momentous a thing as the struggle of love, anger, and jealousy in a soul purely on the evidence set forth here. There is, moreover, an essential falseness about the words. It is hard to believe that Caterina would address herself by name in her thoughts, or refer to herself as "a poor little pale thing," a not very attractive touch of self-pity at best. These things show the author's hand in the description. What is given in this passage is not psychological insight into character, but a flat statement describing an emotional condition rather than revealing it. Instances of this failure to convey the feelings of the characters in dramatic terms are numerous, but a single other example will serve to illustrate the point. Caterina is thinking of Wybrow's marriage and the misery it will cause her:

> "I wish I could be very ill, and die before then," she thought. "When people get very ill, they don't mind about things. . . . O, if I could but like anything—if I could but think about anything else! If these dreadful feelings would go away, I wouldn't mind about not being happy. I wouldn't want anything—and I could do what would please Sir Christopher and Lady Cheverel. But when this rage and anger comes into me, I don't know what to do." (Chapter 11.)

The circumstances surrounding this unspoken soliloquy have a measure of genuine pathos about them, but when Caterina's words are set down so explicitly she becomes self-conscious, and we become aware that we are being appealed to. It is not enough simply to be told a character's thoughts; we must have some picture which will objectify inward feeling. This exposition of Caterina's troubled heart merely shows the surface of her emotional being; we have no real sense of her anguish and therefore are unable to achieve an intimate sympathy with her.

An additional obstacle to our entering into full sympathy with Caterina's suffering is the sentimental attitude which the narrator takes towards her. The opening paragraph of Chapter 3 offers an illustration of this early in the story:

The last chapter has given the discerning reader sufficient insight into the state of things at Cheverel Manor in the summer of 1788. In that summer, we know, the great nation of France was agitated by conflicting thoughts and passions, which were but the beginning of sorrows. And in our Caterina's little breast, too, there were terrible struggles. The poor bird was beginning to flutter and vainly dash its soft breast against the hard iron bars of the inevitable, and we see too plainly the danger, if that anguish should go on heightening instead of being allayed, that the palpitating heart may be fatally bruised.[5]

"Poor" and "little," as might be expected, are the adjectives most frequently applied to Caterina. In the closing paragraphs of Chapter 5, she is called "the poor thing," "this poor little heart," and "our little Tina"; elsewhere she is "the poor little thing," "this poor young soul," and, again and again, "poor child." It has been noted that she thinks of herself as a "poor little pale thing," and she also speaks of herself in this way: "How was it likely," she asks Gilfil concerning Anthony, "he could love me as I loved him? And how could he marry a poor little thing like me?" (Chapter 19.) These are only a few of the dozens of times when "poor" or "little" or both are used in connection with Caterina. Needless to say, this kind of writing defeats its own purpose, for one is soon annoyed at being prodded with the stock vocabulary of sentimentality.

Caterina as a bird is a recurring image in the story. There is something of sentimentality in the metaphor itself, and the language in which it is expressed emphasizes this quality. In the

5. This passage reflects George Eliot's reading during the composition of Part II of "Mr. Gilfil's Love Story." Her journal shows that in January and February she was reading Carlyle's *French Revolution,* and Burke's *Reflections.* The entry for February 1, 1857 (MS, Yale), also notes the reading of *Mansfield Park;* it is interesting to observe a certain similarity between Caterina's position at Cheverel Manor and Fanny Price's at Mansfield Park.

second paragraph of Chapter 3 she is compared to a humming-bird, but generally she is thought of as a song-bird. The following instance is characteristic:

> Alas! you see what jealousy was doing in this poor young soul. Caterina, who had passed her life as a little unobtrusive singing-bird, nestling so fondly under the wings that were outstretched for her, her heart beating only to the peaceful rhythm of love, or fluttering with some easily stifled fear, had begun to know the fierce palpitations of triumph and hatred. (Chapter 5.)

Gilfil also thinks of her as a bird, and if the language of his thoughts is more sentimental still, he at least has the excuse of being in love:

> Caterina would come to love him at last; she would be his. ... How he would cherish her—his little bird with the timid bright eye, and the sweet throat that trembled with love and music! She would nestle against him, and the poor little breast which had been so ruffled and bruised should be safe for evermore. (Chapter 19.)

The bird image is sometimes exchanged for others, but in every case the metaphor is of an easily bruised or wounded living thing. In the following passage it is a hare:

> The poor little thing made her way back, no longer hunger-ing for the cold moist air as a counteractive of inward excite-ment, but with a chill at her heart which made the outward chill only depressing. The golden sunlight beamed through the dripping boughs . . . and the birds were chirping and trilling their new autumnal songs so sweetly, it seemed as if their throats, as well as the air, were all the clearer for the rain; but Caterina moved through all this joy and beauty like a poor wounded leveret painfully dragging its little body

through the sweet clover-tufts—for it, sweet in vain. (Chapter 7.)

In other places, Caterina is described in terms of flowers. We are told that "she grew up very much like the primroses" (Chapter 4) and, in the words of Mr. Bates, the gardener, she is "nesh an' dilicate as a paich-blossom—welly laike a linnet, wi' on'y joost body anoof to hold her voice." (Chapter 4.) When Bates describes Caterina again later, he returns to the imagery of his garden:

"She gets moor nesh an' dilicate than iver," he said, half to himself and half to Hester. "I shouldn't woonder if she fades away, laike them cyclamens as I transplanted. She puts me i' maind on 'em somehow, hangin' on their little thin stalks, so whaite an' tinder." (Chapter 7.)

It is the flower image which prevails in the final descriptions of Caterina. When she at last turns to Gilfil for love and comfort, we are told that "the delicate-tendrilled plant must have something to cling to" (Chapter 20), and when she dies in childbirth, we read that "the delicate plant had been too deeply bruised, and in the struggle to put forth a blossom it died." (Chapter 21.)

The imagery in which the characterization of Caterina is embodied fails to be effective because it is too obviously urged and because the language employed is lacking in freshness and tact. Caterina as a wounded bird or a bruised flower makes too obvious a demand upon our sympathies; the images are so conventional that they preclude our seeing her as a truly human figure with whom we can sympathize without affectation. Nevertheless, this early attempt to suggest character in terms of consistently imagined metaphor is interesting as another foreshadowing of what George Eliot's later work will contain. Here, however, we remain unconvinced of Caterina's reality because she is too patently a literary creation meant to be pathetic. She is pure fabrication, and since George Eliot had no knowledge of her own to bring to the characterization, she gave her heroine the qualities which came most readily to hand from other romantic fiction.

If sentimental is the term which best describes the conception of Caterina, melodramatic best suits her story. The following scene is characteristic of the overwrought manner employed throughout in describing her moments of passion. Unable to bear seeing Wybrow flirt with Miss Assher, Caterina rushes away from the drawing room:

> Outside, she took a candle, and, hurrying along the passages and up the stairs to her own room, locked the door.
>
> "O, I cannot bear it, I cannot bear it!" the poor thing burst out aloud, clasping her little fingers, and pressing them back against her forehead, as if she wanted to break them.
>
> Then she walked hurriedly up and down the room.
>
> "And this must go on for days and days, and I must see it."
>
> She looked about nervously for something to clutch. There was a muslin kerchief lying on the table; she took it up and tore it into shreds as she walked up and down, and then pressed it into hard balls in her hand.
>
> "Oh, it is cruel, it is cruel!" she burst out again aloud, as all those love-moments in the past returned upon her. Then the tears gushed forth, she threw herself on her knees by the bed, and sobbed bitterly. (Chapter 5.)

The words and gestures here are so conventional that it is impossible to feel that any real anguish is involved. Perhaps people do shred kerchiefs and say banal things twice over at moments of stress in real life—and for that reason the words and gestures have become trite; but the thing has been seen so often on the stage and read so often in romantic fiction that it has lost all power to move the spectator.

The passage in which there is implied a comparison between the French Revolution and the "terrible struggles" in "our little Caterina's breast" has been mentioned previously. A similar passage, also obviously reflecting George Eliot's reading of Carlyle, closes the chapter in which the bit of melodrama quoted above appears:

> While this poor little heart was being bruised with a weight too heavy for it, Nature was holding on her calm inexorable way, in unmoved and terrible beauty. The stars were rushing in their eternal courses; the tides swelled to the level of the last expectant week; the sun was making brilliant day to busy nations on the other side of the swift earth. The stream of human thought and deed was hurrying and broadening onward. The astronomer was at his telescope; the great ships were labouring over the waves; the toiling eagerness of commerce, the fierce spirit of revolution, were only ebbing in brief rest; and sleepless statesmen were dreading the possible crisis of the morrow. What were our little Tina and her trouble in this mighty torrent, rushing from one awful unknown to another? Lighter than the smallest centre of quivering life in the water-drop, hidden and uncared for as the pulse of anguish in the breast of the tiniest bird that has fluttered down to its nest with the long-sought food, and has found the nest torn and empty. (Chapter 5.)

This seems to be an attempt to invest Caterina's story with profound philosophical significance. Any such attempt must fail because the story is too slight to bear a weighty message. This single reflection upon cosmic indifference, moreover, is totally unintegrated with the mainstream of the narrative. While "Mr. Gilfil's Love Story" is not without importance as an expression of George Eliot's thought, it cannot be considered an expression of the human condition in terms which would justify the rhetorical, oratorical style employed here.

As might be expected, the style goes most astray as the melodrama nears its climax. The passage in which Caterina takes the dagger from the collection of armor at Cheverel Manor and rushes to meet Wybrow in the woods, only to find him lying dead, is perhaps the worst bit of writing George Eliot ever did:

> See how she rushes noiselessly, like a pale meteor, along the passages and up the gallery stairs! Those gleaming eyes, those bloodless lips, that swift silent tread, make her look like the incarnation of a fierce purpose, rather than a woman. The mid-day sun is shining on the armour in the gallery, making mimic suns on bossed sword-hilts and the angles of polished breastplates. Yes, there are sharp weapons in the gallery. There is a dagger in that cabinet; she knows it well. And as a dragon-fly wheels in its flight to alight for an instant on a leaf, she darts to the cabinet, takes out the dagger, and thrusts it into her pocket. (Chapter 13.)

The language becomes frenzied as Caterina approaches the rendezvous:

> She has reached the Rookery, and is under the gloom of the interlacing boughs. Her heart throbs as if it would burst her bosom—as if every next leap must be its last. Wait, wait, O heart! till she has done this one deed. He will be there— he will be before her in a moment. He will come towards her with that false smile, thinking she does not know his baseness—she will plunge that dagger into his heart.

There follows an attempt to wring the maximum of sympathy from the reader:

> Poor child! poor child! she who used to cry to have the fish put back into the water—who never willingly killed the smallest living thing—dreams now, in the madness of her passion, that she can kill the man whose very voice unnerves her.

The attempt made here to invest Caterina with the most poignant pathos fails completely, because the triteness of the reference to her tender-heartedness destroys whatever sincerity there may be in the passage. In the final clause, moreover, we are amused at the implication, no less funny for being inadvertent, that Caterina could kill Wybrow if he were not so devastatingly attractive. The melodramatic style of the passage reaches a crescendo in the concluding sentences:

> But what is that lying among the dank leaves on the path three yards before her?
> Good God! it is he—lying motionless—his hat fallen off. He is ill, then—he has fainted. Her hand lets go the dagger, and she rushes towards him. His eyes are fixed; he does not see her. She sinks down on her knees, takes the dear head in her arms, and kisses the cold forehead.
> "Anthony, Anthony! speak to me—it is Tina—speak to me! O God, he is dead!"

This scene, from the moment the narration shifts into the present tense, might serve as a compendium of the clichés of sensational romantic fiction in both style and language. It should be noted, however, that some trouble has been taken to prepare for this part of the story. Caterina's wild temper and Anthony's weak heart have been referred to repeatedly previous to this scene, and a hint of what Caterina might be capable of in the circumstances had been carefully planted in an early chapter when, concerning her early years at Cheverel Manor, we are told that

> the little southern bird had its northern nest lined with tenderness, and caresses, and pretty things. A loving sensitive nature was too likely, under such nurture, to have its susceptibility heightened into unfitness for an encounter with any harder experience; all the more, because there were gleams of fierce resistance to any discipline that had a harsh or unloving aspect. For the only thing in which Caterina showed

any precocity was a certain ingenuity in vindictiveness. (Chapter 4.)

This attempt to lay a psychological groundwork for Caterina's future behavior, however, helps but little to make the climactic scene believable; the manner in which the scene is described is too conventionally melodramatic for one to have much faith in the reality of the action. The surprising thing, however, is not that the attempt fails, but that it should have been made at all. If this were the work of just another magazine author catering to the popular taste for romance and melodrama, the thrilling action would have been felt sufficient in itself. The same is true of the central situation, the love triangle of Wybrow, Caterina, and Gilfil. George Eliot, however, devotes the whole of Chapter 4 to tracing the roots of the situation to their origins in the childhood circumstances and early personalities of the three characters. Though the performance is not impressive, it does show that from the beginning of her career George Eliot was concerned with creating situations which grow naturally from a combination of character and circumstance, and with drawing characters who are something more than puppets of the author's imagination.

Nevertheless, in comparison to the simple humor and pathos of "Amos Barton," "Mr. Gilfil's Love Story" seems artificial and contrived. The elements which give the story an overly literary quality—the stately setting, the conventionalized characters, the sentimentalized heroine, the melodramatic style of the narrative— make it impossible to believe in Caterina and her troubles as we can believe in Amos Barton and his. At best, "Mr. Gilfil's Love Story" has the charm of an old romance. John Blackwood predicted that Mr. Gilfil would be more generally popular than Amos Barton, and he was probably right. Most of the reviewers preferred this to the other stories, and a number of later critics have followed their example. Leslie Stephen calls it "almost faultless, and as admirable a specimen of the literary genus to which it belongs as was ever written."[6] A more modern reader abandons all qualification and declares it "the one flawless thing George Eliot ever wrote," and says, with more enthusiasm than discernment, that it "contains not a single weak expression, not a single trite reflection: it is pure gold."[7] F. R. Leavis finds in it "the atmospheric richness of the past seen through home tradition and the associations of childhood," and considers it the only one of the *Scenes* superior to what "might have appeared in any Victorian family magazine."[8] One can account for such opinions only by noting that the story, read uncritically, does leave a general impression of old-fashioned grace and elegance. In addition, there are occasional passages of compelling beauty which one remembers with pleasure after the clichés of sentimentality and melodrama have ceased to annoy. The opening of Chapter 5, for instance, seems to me George Eliot at her best:

> The inexorable ticking of the clock is like the throb of pain to sensations made keen by a sickening fear. And so it is with the great clockwork of nature. Daisies and buttercups give way to the brown waving grasses, tinged with the warm red sorrel; the waving grasses are swept away, and the meadows lie like emeralds set in the bushy hedgerows; the tawny-tipped corn begins to bow with the weight of the full ear; the reapers are bending amongst it, and it soon stands in sheaves; then, presently, the patches of yellow stubble lie side by side with streaks of dark-red earth, which the plough is turning up in preparation for the new-threshed seed. And this passage from beauty to beauty, which to the happy is

6. *George Eliot*, p. 58.
7. May, *George Eliot*, pp. 80–81.
8. *The Great Tradition* (London, 1948), pp. 35–36.

like the flow of a melody, measures for many a human heart the approach of foreseen anguish—seems hurrying on the moment when the shadow of dread will be followed up by the reality of despair.

Despite such loveliness, however, one is inclined to agree with George Eliot herself, when she writes to Blackwood: "I can't help standing up for 'Amos' as better than 'Gilfil.' " (*Letters, 2,* 335.) She gives no reason for this preference, but it seems certain that with her intense devotion to truth in art, she would see in "Amos Barton" a more realistic, a more truly touching picture of human life than in "Mr. Gilfil's Love Story."

Considered as an experiment, the story is of interest for what it shows of George Eliot's limitations when she departed from the material with which she was most familiar. Throughout *Scenes of Clerical Life* she is learning her craft, and it is as important to learn what one cannot do as what one can. It is significant that she did not return to so aristocratic a setting as Cheverel Manor until *Felix Holt* (1866), years later when she was much surer of her powers, and that she never again dealt so exclusively with upper-class characters. "Mr. Gilfil's Love Story," while not an absolute failure, at any rate served to indicate that what she called her "artistic bent" did not lie within the stately confines of Cheverel Manor. It should be remembered, however, that while this story seems to us very inferior George Eliot, it nevertheless had a depth, even in the midst of melodrama, unusual in its day. As noted elsewhere, Lewes saw in it a "subtle truth in delineation of complex motives," and in the characterization of Wybrow and Caterina there is some support for his finding. Yet the fact remains that when we look today for indications of George Eliot's genius in this story we return to the talk of Mrs. Parrot and Mrs. Higgins, to Cross Farm, and to the gentle reflective sadness of the epilogue. These are the things which suggest most surely that the author of "Mr. Gilfil's Love Story" has the qualities of a great novelist.

"JANET'S REPENTANCE":
"The real drama of Evangelicalism"

In "Silly Novels by Lady Novelists," written immediately before she began work on *Scenes of Clerical Life,* George Eliot discusses four types of silly feminine fiction: the *"mind-and-millinery* species," in which the heroine is "usually an heiress, probably a peeress in her own right," who "reads the Bible in the original tongues"; the *"oracular* species—novels intended to expound the writer's religious, philosophical, or moral theories"; the *"modern-antique* species," which deal with "the private love affairs of Sennacherib, or the mental struggles and ultimate conversion of Demetrius the silversmith"; and the *"white neckcloth* species," which represent the tone of thought and feeling in the Evangelical party."[9] Her remarks on this last group cast an interesting light on her own work in "Janet's Repentance."

George Eliot defines the "white neck-cloth" novel as "a kind of genteel tract on a large scale, intended as a sort of medicinal sweetmeat for Low Church young ladies; an Evangelical substitute for the fashionable novel, as the May Meetings are a substitute for the Opera." The characteristics of the species may be inferred from the following comment:

> The Orlando of Evangelical literature is the young curate, looked at from the point of view of the middle class, where cambric bands are understood to have as thrilling an effect on the hearts of young ladies as epaulettes have in the classes above and below it. In the ordinary type of these novels, the hero is almost sure to be a young curate, frowned upon, perhaps, by worldly mammas, but carrying captive the hearts of their daughters, who can "never forget *that* sermon"; tender glances are seized from the pulpit stairs instead of the opera-box; *tête-à-têtes* are seasoned with quotations from

9. *WR,* 66 (October 1856), 442, 449, 458, 456.

Scripture, instead of quotations from the poets; and questions as to the state of the heroine's affections are mingled with anxieties as to the state of her soul. The young curate always has a background of well-dressed and wealthy, if not fashionable society;—for Evangelical silliness is as snobbish as any other kind of silliness.[1]

The stories which George Eliot holds up to scorn here were a development from the novels of purpose that flourished in the eighteen-forties and early fifties.[2] Whether the work of Anglican or Evangelical writers, these tales were concerned only with propagating the doctrinal beliefs of the authors, and were almost totally lacking in narrative interest, to say nothing of narrative skill. Such novels underwent a gradual sophistication of technique, however. The change is indicated in the comment of a contemporary observer who happens to be dealing with Anglo-Catholic fiction but whose words apply equally well to the Evangelical novel:

> By degrees . . . the religious tale dropped its expository conversations and its preachments, and allowed the thread of the story to go on unbroken, trusting to the general tone of the whole to impress the reader with the great practical truths which hang upon, and accompany the belief of doctrinal truths; faith is illustrated more by the life of the character described than by mere theological terms by which it may be expressed.[3]

1. Ibid., p. 456.
2. The most comprehensive modern study of the religious novels of the forties and fifties is Joseph E. Baker, *The Novel and the Oxford Movement* (Princeton, 1932). Kathleen Tillotson discusses religious novels briefly and finds them significant for showing "the growing tendency to introspection in the novel." See *Novels of the Eighteen-Forties* (Oxford, 1954), pp. 125–37.
3. "The Moral Character of Story Books," *Christian Remembrancer*, 40 (July 1860), 61.

From this position, the religious novel easily degenerates into the "white neck-cloth" novel, in which even the indirect illustration of faith is sacrificed to the thread of narrative and only the trappings of religion remain. The novels of which George Eliot writes in the *Westminster* article are actually not religious at all, being at least as closely related to the so-called "silver-fork" novels as to the novel of purpose. A writer in the *Christian Remembrancer* in 1848 had welcomed the religious novel as a better influence in fiction than that of Bulwer-Lytton, whom he called "a westend Adonis," but had hinted at a danger which was to be realized in the development of "white neck-cloth" literature: "Whether another and more fatal humbug may not succeed, and whether a certain phase of the religious novel may not prove that humbug, remains yet to be seen."[4] The particular humbug of the "white neck-cloth" novel is that it pretends to be a picture of life in Evangelical circles, while in fact it is simply, as George Eliot points out, an "evangelical travesty of the fashionable novel." Such books, she says

> remind us of what we sometimes see in a worldly woman recently "converted";—she is as fond of a fine dinner table as before, but she invites clergymen instead of beaux; she thinks as much of her dress as before, but she adopts a more sober choice of colours and patterns; her conversation is as trivial as before, but the triviality is flavoured with gospel instead of gossip.[5]

It is to the element of humbug in the "white neck-cloth" novel that George Eliot objects most strongly. "It is less excusable in an Evangelical novelist, than in any other," she says, "gratuitously to seek her subjects among titles and carriages."[6] Then, speaking

---

4. The statement is made in a review of *Jane Eyre*. *Christian Remembrancer,* *15* (April 1848), 408.
5. *WR, 66* (October 1856), 457.
6. Ibid., p. 457.

with the authority of personal experience, she indicates the proper sphere of the Evangelical novelist:

> The real drama of Evangelicalism—and it has abundance of fine drama for any one who has genius enough to discern and reproduce it—lies among the middle and lower classes; and are not Evangelical opinions understood to give an especial interest in the weak things of the earth, rather than in the mighty? Why then, cannot our Evangelical lady novelists show us the operation of their religious views among people (there really are many such in the world) who keep no carriage, "not so much as a brass-bound gig," who even manage to eat their dinner without a silver fork, and in whose mouths the authoress's questionable English would be strictly consistent? Why can we not have pictures of religious life among the industrial classes in England, as interesting as Mrs. Stowe's pictures of religious life among the negroes?

While George Eliot may have had her own work in mind when she wrote these words, she had said very much the same thing even before the idea of the *Scenes* first occurred to her. In a review in the *Leader* eight months earlier, she had written:

> "Rachel Gray" further professes to show how Christianity exhibits itself as a refining and consoling influence in that most prosaic stratum of society, the small shopkeeping class; and here is really a new sphere for a great artist who can paint from close observation, and who is neither a caricaturist nor a rose-colour sentimentalist.[7]

The emphasis in both these comments upon the connection between social milieu and religion is reflected very clearly in "Janet's Repentance." Much of the interest of the story derives from the

7. *Leader,* January 5, 1856, p. 19.

realistic picture of Milby society which George Eliot draws in the early chapters. Here one sees emerging the organic form which distinguishes her full-length novels. Joan Bennett calls this form "more significant than in any preceding fiction," and describes it as "an inner circle (a small group of individuals involved in a moral dilemma) surrounded by an outer circle (the social world within which the dilemma has to be resolved)."[8] When her art is at its best, as in *Middlemarch,* George Eliot compels our belief in her characters by the success with which she creates the world they live in. The distance between "Janet's Repentance" and *Middlemarch* is immeasurable, but the early experimental story shares with the masterpiece their author's concern with milieu. It is clear from a letter of Lewes' to John Blackwood that George Eliot was perfectly aware of the importance of background in "Janet's Repentance"; she knew, that is, that the credibility of the characters and their story depended upon the success with which she made their world believable. Part I of the magazine version closes with Dempster's drunken abuse of Janet. When Blackwood sent the proof of Part I, he wrote:

> The glimpse at the end of the part shows that a powerful and pathetic story is coming and I rather wish you had plunged sooner into it instead of expending so much humour in the delineation of characters who do not seem likely to assist materially in the movement of the Story and who are not in themselves interesting. (*Letters, 2,* 344.)

George Eliot's reaction to this criticism was expressed through Lewes, who wrote: "I agree with Eliot that it was necessary to paint the locale for the truth of the story. Only in such an atmosphere could such a story move freely and naturally." (*Letters, 2,* 351.) One sees from this that even in her first work George Eliot was consciously striving for the kind of organic form which Mrs. Bennett praises.

8. *George Eliot, Her Mind and Her Art,* p. 101.

Chapter Four

In creating the Milby background of "Janet's Repentance,"
George Eliot combined the function of the artist with that of the
social historian. As social historian she gives a clear and detailed
picture of the town as it might have appeared to a casual observer;
after the comment in the "silly novels" article and the review of
Rachel Gray, it is not surprising to find that she emphasizes the
prosaic surface presented by a community in which the industrial
and small shopkeeping classes predominate: "It was a dingy-
looking town, with a strong smell of tanning up one street and
a great shaking of hand-looms up another; and even in that focus
of aristocracy, Friar's Gate, the houses would not have seemed
very imposing." (Chapter 2.) And again:

> To a superficial glance, Milby was nothing but dreary prose:
> a dingy town, surrounded by flat fields, lopped elms, and
> sprawling manufacturing villages, which crept on and on
> with their weaving-shops, till they threatened to graft them-
> selves on the town. (Chapter 2.)

She gives a vivid sense of the lower-class element in Milby in a
passage leading up to the anti-Tryan "row" preconcerted by
Dempster:

> The Bridge Way was an irregular straggling street, where
> the town fringed off raggedly into the Whitlow road: rows
> of new red-brick houses, in which ribbon-looms were rattling
> behind long lines of windows, alternating with old, half-
> thatched, half-tiled cottages—one of those dismal wide
> streets where dirt and misery have no long shadows thrown
> on them to soften their ugliness. Here, about half-past five
> o'clock, Silly Caleb, an idiot well known in Dog Lane, but
> more of a stranger in the Bridge Way, was seen slouching
> along with a string of boys hooting at his heels; presently
> another group, for the most part out at elbows, came briskly
> in the same direction, looking round them with an air of

expectation; and at no long interval, Deb Traunter, in a pink flounced gown and floating ribbons, was observed talking with great affability to two men in seal-skin caps and fustian, who formed her cortege. The Bridge Way began to have a presentiment of something in the wind. Phib Cook left her evening wash-tub and appeared at her door in soap-suds, a bonnet-poke, and general dampness; three narrow-chested ribbon-weavers, in rusty black streaked with threads of many-coloured silk, sauntered out with their hands in their pockets; and Molly Beale, a brawny old virago, descrying wiry Dame Ricketts peeping out from her entry, seized the opportunity of renewing the morning's skirmish. In short, the Bridge Way was in that state of excitement which is understood to announce a "demonstration" on the part of the British public. (Chapter 4.)

From Deb Traunter and Phib Cook up to the highest that Milby has to offer—which, George Eliot makes clear, is not very high: "there was only one closed carriage in the place, and that was old Mr. Landor's, the banker, who, I think, never drove more than one horse" (Chapter 2)—everyone is named and everyone is put into his exact place in the over-all picture. We are shown the entire social range of a provincial manufacturing town in the England of 1830: the lawyers, Dempster and Pittman; the doctors, Pratt and Pilgrim; the banker, Mr. Landor; the rich miller, Tomlinson, and the rich farmer, Jerome; the provincial dandies, Eustace Landor and Alfred Phipps, and the narrow-chested ribbon-weavers; the belles—Miss Landor, Miss Phipps, and the "Miss Pittmans," " 'finished' at distant and expensive schools"—and the servingmaids. There are old Mr. Crewe, the Anglican curate, and the constantly changing ministers of Dissent at Salem Chapel—Mr. Horner, Mr. Rose, Mr. Stickney, and Mr. Smith. There are Dempster's drinking cronies, Mr. Byles and Mr. Budd, and the Evangelical ladies—the Miss Linnets and their mother, the Miss

153

Pratts, aunt and niece, and Mrs. Pettifer. The list could be extended to great length. All these people, realistically described, and placed not only socially but physically—in Orchard Street or Butcher Lane, in the Bridge Way or on Paddiford Common, in the Red Lion or the Green Man or the Bear and Ragged Staff —create the world in which Janet and Mr. Tryan move. It is pre-eminently the world in which to prove that the "real drama of Evangelicalism lies among the middle and lower classes."

The detailed realism of "Janet's Repentance" reflects, perhaps, a deliberate effort on George Eliot's part to counteract the falsification and sentimentality of such Evangelical fiction as she had derided in "Silly Novels by Lady Novelists," for it seems more carefully worked out and more consciously set forth than simple fidelity would demand. It seemed to John Blackwood that she had gone too far. Concerning the first four chapters of the story, he wrote: "Surely the colours are rather harsh for a sketch of English Country Town life only 25 years ago." (*Letters, 2,* 344.) One does not have to look long to find the "harsh colours" that would trouble John Blackwood: the lawyers are unscrupulous, the doctors are mercenary, the poor are oppressed, the rich are vulgar and pretentious, the whole picture is informed by a suggestion of a generally low moral standard extending from the currier Budd, "whose scandalous life had long furnished his more moral neighbours with an after-dinner joke" (Chapter 1), up to the clergyman, Mr. Crewe:

> The standard of morality at Milby, you perceive, was not inconveniently high in those good old times, and an ingenuous vice or two was what every man expected of his neighbour. Old Mr. Crewe, the curate, for example, was allowed to enjoy his avarice in comfort . . . and his flock liked him all the better for having scraped together a large fortune out of his school and curacy, and the proceeds of the three thousand pounds he had with his little deaf wife. (Chapter 2.)

On the whole, "Janet's Repentance," as published, shows that George Eliot meant what she said when she told Blackwood: "I shall not be able to make any other than *superficial* alterations in the proof." (*Letters, 2,* 347.) But there is some evidence of softening. Concerning drunkenness in Milby we are told that "many of the middle-aged inhabitants, male and female, often found it impossible to keep up their spirits without a very abundant supply of stimulants." (Chapter 2.) Following this, the manuscript reads:

> It is true there were three or four substantial men who had a reputation for exceptional sobriety, and not more than half a dozen married ladies were frequently observed to become less sure of their equilibrium as the day advanced, so Milby habits were really not as bad as possible. (MS fols. 11–12.)[9]

In *Blackwood's* (and in subsequent published versions) the reference to the ladies is omitted. Of Mr. Crewe, the curate, the manuscript records: "His brown wig was hardly ever put on quite right, and sometimes, when he spat, he made noises not in the rubric." (MS fol. 14.) The second half of the sentence is omitted in publication. There is only one passage of any length omitted in the printed version of the story; following a description of Mr. Jerome's good works, which consisted in "loans of money to the ostensibly rich, and in sacks of potatoes to the obviously poor" (Chapter 2), the manuscript (but not the published version) continues:

> That sort of virtue was not common at Milby, in spite of Mr. Dempster's alarm at the introduction of a doctrine which would invalidate the efficacy of good works. The virtue there, I imagine, was chiefly of that negative kind which consists in not pretending to be better than one's neighbours, and in

9. In the MS, each of the five parts of "Janet's Repentance" is numbered from "1," but chapter references in my text will prevent difficulty in finding quotations.

this it might safely challenge comparison with the most ingenuous [?] of provincial towns. Drunkenness was indulged in with great candour; no one put on very charming manners to his wife when in company; neighbours on the best of terms imputed boastful lying and spiteful detraction to each other without any affectation of disgust; and other sins prayed against in the litany were the subject of very free allusion and were committed with considerable openness. Dempster's life, to be sure, was thought too flagrantly irregular; his drinking was out of all bounds, and he often abused his wife beyond what was reasonable. Still he was one of those valuable public characters in whom society has at all times tolerated an extra amount of private aberration; he was very well received in most houses, and there were several ladies rather proud of "knowing how to manage Dempster," or of jocosely twitting him with being a sad husband. (MS fols. 22–23.)

Of "softening" other than by omission, I have found only one instance: an addition to the satirical portrait of the doctor, Mr. Pilgrim. The last sentence in the following passage appears in all published versions but not in the manuscript:

The doctor's estimate, even of a confiding patient, was apt to rise and fall with the entries in the day-book; and I have known Mr. Pilgrim to discover the most unexpected virtues in a patient seized with a promising illness. At such times you might have been glad to perceive that there were some of Mr. Pilgrim's fellow-creatures of whom he entertained a high opinion, and that he was liable to the amiable weakness of a too admiring estimate. A good inflammation fired his enthusiasm, and a lingering dropsy dissolved him into charity. Doubtless this *crescendo* of benevolence was partly due to feelings not at all represented by the entries in the day-book; for in Mr. Pilgrim's heart, too, there was a latent store of

tenderness and pity which flowed forth at the sight of suffering. (Chapter 2; MS fol. 21.)

None of these modifications affects in any significant way the
impression given of Milby in the original manuscript version of
the story. To the objective eye of the social historian, Milby offered
very little of goodness or loveliness, and George Eliot refused to
falsify her picture by seeing good where it did not exist. She knew,
however, that a picture wholly bad would be as false as one
wholly good, and would as surely destroy the credibility of her
study of Evangelicalism. Hence she writes:

Assuredly Milby had that salt of goodness which keeps the
world together, in greater abundance than was visible on the
surface: Innocent babes were born there, sweetening their
parents' hearts with simple joys; men and women withering
in disappointed worldliness, or bloated with sensual ease, had
better moments in which they pressed the hand of suffering
with sympathy, and were moved to deeds of neighbourly
kindness. . . . And so it was with the human life there, which
at first seemed a dismal mixture of griping worldliness, vanity, ostrich feathers, and the fumes of brandy: looking closer,
you found some purity, gentleness, and unselfishness, as you
may have observed a scented geranium giving forth its
wholesome odours amidst blasphemy and gin in a noisy pot-
house. (Chapter 2.)

Like "Amos Barton" and "Mr. Gilfil's Love Story," "Janet's Repentance" is concerned with the drama of humanity which lies
beneath the commonplace (and in this case ugly) surface, but
here, more than in the earlier "scenes," the surface is an integral
part of the drama (as in *The Mill on the Floss* and *Middlemarch*),
and the actors derive their personal reality from the reality of
their environment.

Chapter Four

George Eliot's treatment of the drama of Evangelicalism is one of the most interesting elements in *Scenes of Clerical Life.* She was peculiarly well-qualified to handle this theme, and her picture is interesting not only in itself as a vivid re-creation of the life of the people at one point of their social and religious history, but also as an indication of the mature balance of George Eliot's mind at the time when she began to write fiction. As a novelist, she saw in the drama of Evangelicalism excellent material for an artist whose genius was for realistic portrayal of common life, and it may have been her exasperation with those who treated this material unrealistically which in part prompted her to write "Janet's Repentance." I believe, however, that she also had a reason of much greater personal significance, having to do with her own mental development. She wanted, I think, to set down clearly, with neither bitterness nor sentimentality, her mature feelings about the discarded religion of her youth.

The stages of George Eliot's intellectual development are suggested in Basil Willey's comment:

> Probably no English writer of the time, and certainly no novelist, more fully epitomizes the century; her development is a paradigm, her intellectual biography a graph, of its most decided trend. Starting from evangelical Christianity, the curve passes through doubt to a reinterpreted Christ and a religion of humanity: beginning with God, it ends in Duty.[1]

This says nothing of the emotional attitudes accompanying the development or of the final attitude toward that which had been discarded, of the long antagonism and the ultimate tolerance, but of these things George Eliot herself has written, and one may best see the place of "Janet's Repentance" in her development by bracketing it between an article of 1855 and a letter of 1859. The article is "Evangelical Teaching: Dr. Cumming," published in the *Westminster Review;* the letter, one often quoted, was to her old

1. *Nineteenth Century Studies,* pp. 204–05.

friend, François D'Albert-Durade, at whose house she had lived when she went to Geneva following her father's death in 1849. After reading *Adam Bede,* D'Albert-Durade wrote George Eliot:

> Dans bien des pages je vous ai retrouvée; mais dans d'autres je ne vous eusse certes pas reconnue; quelques années ont-elles amené ces modifications de votre pensée, de vos suppositions sur l'état de l'âme pendant et après cette vie, suppositions qui se rapprochaient un peu du panthéisme, ou bien le tout n'était-il ou n'est-il encore qu'on jeu de votre imagination! (*Letters, 3,* 230n.)

George Eliot was not surprised that there were many pages in *Adam Bede* in which he could not recognize "the 'Marian' or 'Minie' of old Geneva days," and she attempts to explain the difficulty:

> We knew each other too short a time, and I was under too partial and transient a phase of my mental history, for me to pour out to you much of my earlier experience. I think I hardly ever spoke to you of the strong hold Evangelical Christianity had on me from the age of fifteen to two and twenty and of the abundant intercourse I had had with earnest people of various religious sects. When I was at Geneva, I had not yet lost the attitude of antagonism which belongs to the renunciation of *any* belief—also, I was very unhappy, and in a state of discord and rebellion towards my own lot. Ten years of experience have wrought great changes in that inward self: I have no longer any antagonism towards any faith in which human sorrow and human longing for purity have expressed themselves; on the contrary, I have a sympathy with it that predominates over all argumentative tendencies. (*Letters, 3,* 230–31.)

Perhaps the writing of "Janet's Repentance" helped George Eliot to arrive at the tolerant position described here. This is not to say, of course, that she learned tolerance through her writing, but only that the experience of giving concrete expression to an already present tendency of thought enabled her to achieve a clear perspective on her past experience.

Only four years before the letter to D'Albert-Durade her hostility toward Evangelicalism was still active, finding lively expression in the article on Dr. John Cumming, a popular preacher of the time. The article is, to be sure, concerned only with Dr. Cumming, but her statement that "his creed often obliges him to hope the worst of men, and to exert himself in proving that the worst is true,"[2] is an indictment of Evangelicalism generally, and the opening sentences of the article show plainly that George Eliot regarded Cumming as representative of a type:

> Given, a man with moderate intellect, a moral standard not higher than the average, some rhetorical affluence and great glibness of speech, what is the career in which, without the aid of birth or money, he may most easily attain power and reputation in English society? Where is that Goshen of mediocrity in which a smattering of science and learning will pass for profound instruction, where platitudes will be accepted as wisdom, bigoted narrowness as holy zeal, unctuous egoism as God-given piety? Let such a man become an evangelical preacher; he will then find it possible to reconcile small ability with great ambition, superficial knowledge with the prestige of erudition, a middling morale with a high reputation for sanctity.[3]

Lawyer Dempster would have delighted in this article and would have felt that George Eliot's prescription for an Evangelical preacher was perfectly suited in Mr. Tryan. In "Evangelical

2. *WR*, 64 (October 1855), 462.
3. Ibid., pp. 436–37.

Teaching: Dr. Cumming," George Eliot sees only the bad side of Evangelicalism, the cant, hypocrisy, and sanctimoniousness. In "Janet's Repentance," she takes a long, objectively sympathetic look at the popular religion she had discarded fifteen years before, and the result is a full demonstration of the good it can bring into the lives of its adherents. George Eliot never repudiated her contempt for Dr. Cumming,[4] but in "Janet's Repentance" she shows her mature awareness that Evangelicalism can fill a very real need and that it has often been a great force for good.

Mr. Graham Hough's comment on George Eliot's presentation of non-conformist religion in *Adam Bede* and *Felix Holt* may be applied with equal justice to her treatment of Evangelicalism in "Janet's Repentance":

> Very few writers can avoid the allurements of irony or sentimentalism in dealing with a religious background they have themselves outgrown, and perhaps this is why, in spite of the notorious piety of English life, popular Protestantism has had so little justice done to it by English writers. Most of them have been concerned to show that they were clever enough to see through it, or though clever, still good enough to respect it. But George Eliot is quite simply concerned with seeing the object as it really is, without the distortions of ambivalence.[5]

To see Evangelicalism "as it really is" meant seeing the good and bad together, hypocrisy as well as sincerity, absurdity as well as beauty. George Eliot neglects no aspect of the movement: "Religious ideas," she writes, "have the fate of melodies, which, once

4. The article on Cumming is among the essays written before 1857 which Charles Lee Lewes says George Eliot "considered deserving of a permanent form." See his preface to *Essays and Leaves from a Note-Book* (Edinburgh and London, 1884, Vol. 21 of the Cabinet Edition of George Eliot's works).

5. "Novelist-Philosophers: XII—George Eliot," *Horizon*, 17 (January 1948), 56.

set afloat in the world, are taken up by all sorts of instruments, some of them woefully coarse, feeble, or out of tune, until people are in danger of crying out that the melody itself is detestable." (Chapter 10.) With perfect clear-sightedness she presents the case against Evangelicalism:

> It may be that some of Mr. Tryan's hearers had gained a religious vocabulary rather than a religious experience; that here and there a weaver's wife, who, a few months before, had been simply a silly slattern, was converted into that more complex nuisance, a silly and sanctimonious slattern; that the old Adam, with the pertinacity of middle age, continued to tell fibs behind the counter notwithstanding the new Adam's addiction to Bible reading and family prayer . . . and that at Milby, in those distant days, as in all other times and places where the mental atmosphere is changing, and men are inhaling the stimulus of new ideas, folly often mistook itself for wisdom, ignorance gave itself airs of knowledge, and selfishness, turning its eyes upward, called itself religion. (Chapter 10.)

Besides recognizing the hypocrisy which may attend Evangelical "conversion," George Eliot can laugh at the pietism of the women who form an admiring circle around Mr. Tryan. There is Mrs. Linnet, for instance, who had become a reader of religious books since Mr. Tryan's advent:

> On taking up the biography of a celebrated preacher, she immediately turned to the end to see what disease he died of; and if his legs swelled, as her own occasionally did, she felt a stronger interest in ascertaining any earlier facts in the history of the dropsical divine. . . . She then glanced over the letters and diary, and wherever there was a predominance of Zion, the River of Life, and notes of exclamation, she turned over to the next page. (Chapter 3.)

The spinster Miss Linnets, in "that temperate zone of old-maidism, when a woman will not say but that if a man of suitable years and character were to offer himself, she might be induced to tread the remainder of life's vale in company with him" (Chapter 3), tremble with pleasurable agitation whenever Mr. Tryan comes near. Funniest of all is Miss Pratt, Milby's one blue-stocking, whose published works include *Letters to a Young Man on his Entrance to Life,* and *De Courcy, or the Rash Promise, a Tale for Youth.* Her "latest production had been Six Stanzas, addressed to the Rev. Edgar Tryan, printed on glazed paper with a neat border, and beginning, 'Forward, young wrestler for the truth!' " (Chapter 3.) In the conversation of Miss Pratt, George Eliot recaptures exactly the tone and accent of her own early letters. Miss Pratt's remarks on the Paddiford Lending Library are typical:

> "It is a most admirable selection of works for popular reading, this that our excellent Mr. Tryan has made. I do not know whether, if the task had been confided to me, I could have made a selection combining in a higher degree religious instruction and edification, with a due admixture of the purer species of amusement. . . . I have ever considered fiction a suitable form for conveying moral and religious instruction." (Chapter 3.)

Miss Pratt would have delighted in a correspondent like the eighteen-year-old Mary Ann Evans who writes to her friend Miss Lewis:

> I do not wonder you are pleased with Pascal; his thoughts may be returned to the palate again and again with increasing rather than diminished relish. I have highly enjoyed Hannah More's letters; the contemplation of so blessed a character as hers is very salutary. (*Letters, 1, 7.*)

But though George Eliot sees the hypocrisy which sometimes attends Evangelicalism, and though she can laugh at some of the

effects which Mr. Tryan produces, she realizes that these things
are insignificant in comparison with the real good accomplished
by the movement. The good she is concerned with, however, is
not the public philanthropic aspect embodied in the work of
Wilberforce or Hannah More or the missionary societies. Still less
is she concerned with the possible good to be derived from an
acceptance of particular points of Evangelical doctrine. She is
concerned, rather, with showing that Evangelical enthusiasm can
touch "the spring of goodness" in ordinary lives and make people
better in the simplest but most fundamental things of life, that
it can awaken a higher sense of duty and stir impulses of selflessness in the hearts of men. The following passage is a full statement of George Eliot's attitude toward the religion of her youth;
free from both irony and sentimentality, it is the most detailed
and concretely illustrated expression to be found in her writings
of her mature view of Evangelical Christianity. The passage
illuminates, and perhaps even helped to make possible, George
Eliot's statement to M. D'Albert-Durade: "I have no longer any
antagonism towards any faith in which human sorrow and human
longing for purity have expressed themselves."

> Evangelicalism had brought into palpable existence and
> operation in Milby society that idea of duty, that recognition
> of something to be lived for beyond the mere satisfaction of
> self, which is to the moral life what the addition of a great
> central ganglion is to animal life. No man can begin to
> mould himself on a faith or an idea without rising to a higher
> order of experience: a principle of subordination, of self-
> mastery, has been introduced into his nature; he is no longer
> a mere bundle of impressions, desires, and impulses. What-
> ever might be the weaknesses of the ladies who pruned the
> luxuriance of their lace and ribbons, cut out garments for
> the poor, distributed tracts, quoted Scripture, and defined the
> true Gospel, they had learned this—that there was a divine

work to be done in life, a rule of goodness higher than the opinion of their neighbours; and if the notion of a heaven in reserve for themselves was a little too prominent, yet the theory of fitness for that heaven consisted in purity of heart, in Christ-like compassion, in the subduing of selfish desires. They might give the name of piety to much that was only puritanic egoism; they might call many things sin that were not sin; but they had at least the feeling that sin was to be avoided and resisted, and colour-blindness, which may mistake drab for scarlet, is better than total blindness, which sees no distinction of colour at all. Miss Rebecca Linnet, in quiet attire, with a somewhat excessive solemnity of countenance, teaching at the Sunday-school, visiting the poor, and striving after a standard of purity and goodness, had surely more moral loveliness than in those flaunting peony-days, when she had no other model than the costumes of the heroines in the circulating library. Miss Eliza Pratt, listening in rapt attention to Mr. Tryan's evening lecture, no doubt found evangelical channels for vanity and egoism; but she was clearly in moral advance of Miss Phipps giggling under her feathers at old Mr. Crewe's peculiarities of enunciation. And even elderly fathers and mothers, with minds, like Mrs. Linnet's, too tough to imbibe much doctrine, were the better for having their hearts inclined towards the new preacher as a messenger from God. They became ashamed, perhaps, of their evil tempers, ashamed of their worldliness, ashamed of their trivial, futile past. The first condition of human goodness is something to love; and second, something to reverence. And this latter precious gift was brought to Milby by Mr. Tryan and Evangelicalism. (Chapter 10.)[6]

6. George Eliot's discussion of Evangelicalism in "Janet's Repentance" illuminates the comment of historians of the movement. See for instance Justin McCarthy's remarks on the effects of Wesley's and Whitefield's teachings: "They inspired the soul of the poor and commonplace creatures with all the

In the above passage, George Eliot is mainly concerned with the moral effect of Evangelicalism; "Janet's Repentance" also gives a vivid picture of the social impact of the movement, and is thus connected with the larger design of *Scenes of Clerical Life* as a whole. Taken together, the three stories provide an illuminating footnote to the social history of provincial English religious life in the first four decades of the nineteenth century.

"Mr. Gilfil's Love Story" presents the old high-and-dry orthodoxy of the eighteenth century which lingered on unchanged in such remote parishes as Shepperton (and in Mary Ann Evans' Chilvers Coton). The young Gilfil is a clergyman of the type found in Jane Austen's novels, a man for whom ordination is simply the instrument through which one achieves one's particular place in society. Sir Christopher Cheverel's attitude toward Gilfil illustrates the essential character of the type:

> Sir Christopher satisfied several feelings in installing Maynard as chaplain in his house. He liked the old-fashioned dignity of that domestic appendage; he liked his ward's companionship; and, as Maynard had some private fortune, he might take life easily in that agreeable home, keeping his hunter, and observing a mild regimen of clerical duty, until Cumbermoor living should fall in, when he might be settled for life in the neighbourhood of the manor. ("Mr. Gilfil's Love Story," Chapter 4.)

---

zealot's fire and the martyr's endurance. . . . They pierced through the dull, vulgar, contaminated hideousness of low and vicious life, and sent streaming in upon it the light of a higher world and a better law." (*A History of the Four Georges* [4 vols. New York, 1890], 2, 145.) Canon Overton, the High Church historian, writes: "Of the faith which . . . made the selfish man self-denying, the discontented happy, the worldling spiritually-minded, the drunkard sober, the sensual chaste, the liar truthful, the proud humble, the godless godly, the thriftless thrifty, we can only judge by the fruits which it bore. That such fruits *were* borne is surely undeniable." (J. H. Overton, *The Evangelical Revival* [London, 1891], p. 131.)

As vicar of Shepperton, Mr. Gilfil does not trouble his parishioners
with doctrine or theology—"He had a large heap of short sermons,
rather yellow and worn at the edges, from which he took two
every Sunday, securing perfect impartiality in the selection by
taking them as they came, without reference to topics" (Chapter
1)—and his parishioners respected him "as a gentleman and a
clergyman" (the order is significant). No question concerning his
beliefs or the spiritual nature of his office would ever arise in their
minds: "The Knebley farmers would as soon have thought of
criticising the moon as their pastor. He belonged to the course of
nature, like markets and tollgates and dirty bank-notes." (Chapter 1.)

Mr. Gilfil died in 1827.[7] The action of "Amos Barton" takes
place ten years later,[8] or "after an interval in which Evangelicalism and the Catholic Question had begun to agitate the rustic
mind with controversial debates" ("Amos Barton," Chapter 1)
and when "the effect of the Tractarian agitation was beginning
to be felt in backward provincial regions" (Chapter 2):

> A zealous evangelical preacher had made the old sounding-
> board vibrate with quite a different sort of elocution from
> Mr. Gilfil's; the hymn-book had almost superseded the Old
> and New Versions; and the great square pews were crowded
> with new faces from distant corners of the parish—perhaps
> from dissenting chapels. (Chapter 1.)[9]

7. The date is inferred from the opening sentence of the story: "When old
Mr. Gilfil died, thirty years ago, etc."

8. Chap. 6 contains a reference to "the immense sale of the 'Pickwick Papers,' recently completed."

9. A. Dwight Culler notes that the connection between Evangelical Churchmen and Dissenters "was not limited to their common impulse in the Wesleyan
movement but extended to the interchange of good offices and even to the
passing back and forth between them of individual members." (Introduction
to Newman's *Apologia Pro Vita Sua* [Boston, 1956], p. xv.) Mr. Jerome, in
"Janet's Repentance," is a case in point.

Chapter Four

Clearly a great change has taken place between the time of Mr. Gilfil and that of Amos Barton. "Janet's Repentance" is concerned with one aspect of this change—the coming of Evangelicalism.

Before Mr. Tryan's arrival in Milby, there is very little enthusiasm for any sort of religion in this provincial backwater. The Church is taken for granted and has ceased to have any vital connection with the lives of the people. The point is made clear in the narrator's ironic comments about the curate and about churchgoing habits. Since there were "several substantial men who had a reputation for exceptional sobriety," we are told, "Milby habits were really not as bad as possible; and no one is warranted in saying that old Mr. Crewe's flock could not have been worse without any clergyman at all." (Chapter 2.) Or again:

> The well-dressed parishioners generally were very regular church-goers, and to the younger ladies and gentlemen I am inclined to think that the Sunday morning service was the most exciting event of the week; for few places could present a more brilliant show of out-door toilettes. (Chapter 2.)

The statement made later in the story that the second condition of human goodness—namely, something to reverence—was the "precious gift" brought to Milby by Mr. Tryan and Evangelicalism, has full significance only in reference to the attitude toward Mr. Crewe described in Chapter 2. "There was almost always something funny about old Mr. Crewe," the narrator remarks:

> His brown wig was hardly ever put on quite right, and he had a way of raising his voice for three or four words, and lowering it again to a mumble, so that we could scarcely make out a word he said; though, as my mother observed, that was of no consequence in the prayers, since everyone

168

had a prayer-book; and as for the sermon . . . we all of us
heard more of it than we could remember when we got home.

In the same chapter we are told: "It is true he was not spoken of
in terms of highest respect," and "The parishioners saw no reason
at all why it should be desirable to venerate the parson or any one
else: They were much more comfortable to look down a little on
their fellow-creatures." Non-conformity has no more vitality than
the established religion:

> Even the Dissent in Milby was then of a lax and indifferent
> kind. The doctrine of adult baptism, struggling under a
> heavy load of debt, had let off half its chapel area as a ribbon-
> shop; and Methodism was only to be detected, as you detect
> curious larvae, by diligent search in dirty corners. (Chapter
> 2.)

With the installation of Mr. Tryan as curate at the chapel-of-
ease on Paddiford Common, all this is changed: "The rumour
sprang up that Evangelicalism had invaded Milby parish;—a
murrain or blight all the more terrible, because its nature was but
dimly conjectured." (Chapter 2.) George Eliot's picture of the state
of affairs into which Milby is thrown by his arrival has genuine
historical value. It is a piece of social reporting which bypasses
discussion of the doctrinal disputes within the Church of England
to show the working out in ordinary life of the effects of those
disputes. It is a vivid picture of the ignorance and virulence which
find popular expression in times of great social change. Doctrinal
considerations are a part of the background. In the first chapter,
Dempster rants about Mr. Tryan's "sectarian, antinomian, ana-
baptist doctrine" (meaning his preaching against justification by
works), while on the other side Miss Pratt speaks piously of justification by faith, "that cardinal doctrine of the Reformation"
(Chapter 3); and Mr. Tryan precipitates the controversy in the

parish by charging that "old Mr. Crewe did not preach the Gospel" (Chapter 2), thus pinning his attack on a specific point of Evangelical belief.[1] All this is important in the story, but it is the social aspect of Evangelicalism which occupies the foreground. In the following passage, we see clearly that it is mainly as a social force that Evangelicalism is considered a "murrain or blight":

Mr. Tryan was the first Evangelical clergyman who had risen above the Milby horizon: hitherto that obnoxious adjective had been unknown to the townspeople of any gentility. . . . As long as Mr. Tryan's hearers were confined to Paddiford Common—which, by the by, was hardly recognisable as a common at all, but was a dismal district where you heard the rattle of the handloom, and breathed the smoke of coal-pits—the "canting parson" could be treated as a joke. Not so when a number of single ladies in town appeared to be infected, and even one or two men of substantial property . . . seemed to be "giving in" to the new movement—when Mr. Tryan was known to be well received in several good houses, where he was in the habit of finishing the evening with exhortation and prayer. Evangelicalism was no longer a nuisance existing merely in by-corners which any well-clad person could avoid; it was invading the very drawing-rooms, mingling itself with the comfortable fumes of port-wine and brandy, threatening to deaden with its murky breath all the splendour of the ostrich feathers, and to stifle Milby ingenuousness, not pretending to be better than its neighbours, with a cloud of cant and lugubrious hyprocrisy. (Chapter 2.)

1. The *OED* defines "Evangelical" as the "school of Protestants which maintains that the essence of 'the Gospel' consists in the doctrine of salvation by faith in the atoning work of Christ, and denies that either good works or the sacraments have any saving efficacy." ("Evangelical," 2b.) G. W. E. Russell calls this definition "a sound epitome of Evangelical teaching." (*A Short History of the Evangelical Movement* [London, 1915], p. 7.)

Social considerations also make the relationship between Evangelicalism and Dissent, embodied in Mr. Tryan, so hateful to the bigoted orthodoxy of Dempster and his circle. Mr. Tomlinson's gravest charge against him is that he "preaches without book, just like a Dissenter." (Chapter 1.) "Evangelicals," says Luke Byles, "are not Churchmen at all; they're no better than Presbyterians," whom Dempster defines as the "brood of Dissenting vermin that crawl about in dirty alleys." (Chapter 1.) This definition is related to the statement made in the next chapter that "Methodism was only to be detected, as you detect curious larvae, by diligent search in dirty corners." Clearly, the orthodox Milby mind considers Dissent generally no religion for a gentleman. Mr. Tryan, who is, according to Miss Pratt, "of a highly respectable family indeed, in Huntingdonshire" and "quite *comme il faw*", presents a puzzle:

It was a great anomaly to the Milby mind that a canting evangelical parson, who would take tea with tradespeople, and make friends of vulgar women like the Linnets, should have so much the air of a gentleman, and be so little like the splay-footed Mr. Stickney of Salem, to whom he approximated so closely in doctrine. And this want of correspondence between the physique and the creed had excited no less surprise in the larger town of Laxeter, where Mr. Tryan had formerly held a curacy; for of the two other Low Church clergymen in the neighbourhood, one was a Welshman of globose figure and unctuous complexion, and the other a man of atrabiliar aspect, with lank black hair, and a redundance of limp cravat—in fact, the sort of thing you might expect in men who distributed the publications of the Religious Tract Society, and introduced Dissenting hymns into the Church. (Chapter 3.)

In her picture of Milby, George Eliot stresses the backwardness of the region, and it is important to bear this in mind in considering the social character of the anti-Tryanite feeling. Only in such an unenlightened area could Dempster, in 1829–30, have marshaled so much support in the cause of reaction. As Dean Carpenter notes: "Where ignorance reigned supreme, the sophistry of a Dempster could still appeal to the prejudice of an unreasoning conservatism, but the towns had been disillusioned."[2] In a place like Milby, however, "one of the last spots to be reached by the wave of a new movement" (Chapter 2), any innovation is apt to be regarded with hostility, especially if it is of the sort which threatens widespread change, and change was an inevitable result of the acceptance of practical Evangelicalism: the main characteristic of the Evangelical school, says Gladstone, "was a strong, systematic, outspoken, and determined reaction against the prevailing standards both of life and preaching."[3] It is the prevailing standard—the social status quo—which Dempster's party is bent on preserving, not the doctrinal position of the Church of England, of which they can have no very accurate conception. They see in Evangelicalism, with its concern for the lower classes and its essentially democratic doctrine (to say nothing of its intense moral earnestness), a serious threat to their own security. The first words of the story are Dempster's denunciation of the introduction of "demoralizing" doctrine into the parish, and the remarks of his friend Mr. Tomlinson show what kind of demoralization is meant:

> "Well! I'll not stick at giving *my*self trouble to put down such hypocritical cant," said Mr. Tomlinson, the rich miller. "I know well enough what your Sunday-evening lectures are good for—for wenches to meet their sweethearts, and brew mischief. There's work enough with the servant-maids as it is—such as I never heard the like of in my mother's time, and it's all along o' your schooling and newfangled plans."

2. S. C. Carpenter, *Church and People, 1789–1889* (London, 1937), p. 57.
3. *Gleanings of Past Years* (7 vols. New York, 1879), 7, 207.

Dempster's ignorant calumny of the "brood of Dissenting vermin" culminates in his charge that they "circumvent the lord of the manor in order to get a few yards of ground for their pigeon-house conventicles." Dissent is most dangerous because it produces in the lower classes an awareness of the evils of their position: "John Presbyter," the founder of Presbyterianism according to Dempster, is most to be despised for "inoculating the vulgar with the asinine virus of Dissent." Social innovation, then, not doctrinal belief, is the true object of hatred.

George Eliot told Blackwood that "Janet's Repentance," "so far as regards the *persecution,* is a real bit in the religious history of England." (*Letters, 2,* 347.) In the story itself, she reproduces in full Dempster's broadside attack on Tryan (in the mock playbill) on the grounds that it "ought by all means to be preserved amongst the materials of our provincial religious history." (Chapter 9.) In reading the story one does indeed have the sense of actual historical truth. There can be little doubt that Dempster's rabble-rousing is a faithful picture of the methods and attitudes of popular opposition to the Evangelical movement. For instance, the playbill which he and Janet get up to ridicule Mr. Tryan indicates vividly the main attributes which ignorance and bigotry, supported in many cases by church authorities,[4] ascribed to Evangelical preachers. The title of Dempster's "Grand Entertainment" is *The Wolf in Sheep's Clothing or the Methodist in a Mask.* This title is an accurate reflection of a central idea in anti-Evangelical literature. In one of the most widely circulated tracts of the period, listed for twenty-six years (1803–29) in the catalogue of the

4. Gladstone, writing in 1879 of "the experience of half a century ago," notes: "Nothing could be sharper than was, at that time, the animosity of Churchmen in general against what are termed Evangelical opinions. There was language used about them and their proposers in works of authority—such, for instance, as certain tracts of the Society for Promoting Christian Knowledge—which was not only insolent, but almost libellous." (*Gleanings of Past Years, 6,* 157–58.)

Society for Promoting Christian Knowledge, Dr. Thomas Sikes, the Vicar of Guilsborough, declares that the worst thing about the Evangelical clergy is that they are traitors to their own church: "The dissenting teacher stands upon his ground with honour, and acts neither artfully nor falsely," but the Evangelical "plays the hypocrite in a most shocking manner; he receives the Bishop's ordination which puts him into the Church, and then acts directly in opposition to it."[5] This is the view which Dempster spreads with regard to Mr. Tryan's position in Milby.

The playbill also reveals the conception held in some Church circles of the hypocrisy, sanctimoniousness, and ambition of the Evangelical clergy. The hypothetical entertainment is to conclude with "a screaming farce of *The Pulpit Snatcher,*" and the names of the characters—all to be played by Mr. Tryan (here called "Mr. Try-it-on") suggest more vividly than scholarly religious histories can, the qualities commonly attributed to Evangelical preachers: Mr. Saintly Smooth-face and Mr. Malevolent Prayerful, suggesting sanctimoniousness and hypocrisy; Mr. All-grace No-works and Mr. Elect-and-Chosen Apewell, touching on doctrinal heresies; and Mr. Worming Snaker, Mr. Foist-himself-Everywhere, and Mr. Flout-the-aged Upstart, reflecting the supposed ambition of Evangelicals.

Historically true also is Dempster's method of manipulating the mob, which he incites to demonstrate against Mr. Tryan. His main tactic is to assemble "two knots of picked men—one to feed the flame of orthodox zeal with gin-and-water, at the Green Man . . . the other to solidify their church principles with heady beer at the Bear and Ragged Staff." (Chapter 4.) Dempster is only following the example of the Lancashire curate who, in the time of the Wesleys, issued the following proclamation:

5. *A Dialogue between a Minister of the Church and His Parishioner concerning Those Who are Called Gospel Preachers or Evangelical Ministers* (London, 1804), p. 61.

If any man be mindful to enlist under the command of the Rev. George White for the defence of the Church of England, let him repair to the cross, where he shall have a pint of ale in advance and other proper encouragements.[6]

Dempster also provides "proper encouragements." His inflammatory address to the mob is a lively re-creation of anti-Evangelical feeling. From this speech as from the playbill, one may infer the nature of the charges commonly levelled against the Evangelical clergy. After flattering the crowd ("Your hearts are sound to the core! No man had better try to thrust his cant and hypocrisy down *your* throats"), Dempster moves on to a vituperative enumeration of Evangelical infamy:

"Yes, my fellow Townsmen! I have the gratification of announcing to you thus formally what you have already learned indirectly. The pulpit from which our venerable pastor has fed us with sound doctrine for half a century is not to be invaded by a fanatical, sectarian, double-faced, Jesuitical interloper! We are not to have our young people demoralised and corrupted by the temptations to vice, notoriously connected with Sunday evening lectures! We are not to have a preacher obtruding himself upon us, who decries good works, and sneaks into our homes perverting the faith of our wives and daughters! We are not to be poisoned with doctrines which damp every innocent enjoyment, and pick a poor man's pocket of the six-pence with which he might buy himself a cheerful glass after a hard day's work, under the pretence of paying for bibles to send to the Chicktaws!" (Chapter 4.)

The evils which Dempster proclaims here may all be found as subjects of actual tracts circulated in England in the early decades of the nineteenth century.

6. William Miles, *The Life and Writings of William Grimshaw* (Newcastle, 1906), p. 114.

Graham Hough has said that "if we really want to know what it felt like to live in pre-Reform Bill England," we must go to *Felix Holt* or *Middlemarch*.[7] A similar statement could be made of "Janet's Repentance": if we really want to know what the coming of Evangelicalism meant in provincial English life, we can probably do no better than to turn to the third of the *Scenes of Clerical Life*. The story has serious defects—we do not really believe in Janet's alcoholism; there are moments of crude sentimentality (as when, in connection with Janet's sorrows, attention is directed to Janet's mother in Chapter 4: "Poor grey-haired woman! Was it for this you suffered a mother's pangs in your lone widowhood five-and-thirty years ago?"); and it is surely a mistake to have Mr. Tryan fall in love with Janet at the end of the story. But in the delineation of the background and in the staging of the drama of Evangelicalism there is no false touch. In the early chapters of "Janet's Repentance" George Eliot gives good earnest of one of her most valuable assets as a novelist—the ability to construct a social setting which creates and is at the same time created by the people whose milieu it is. In 1860, with *Adam Bede* behind her and most of *The Mill on the Floss* written, George Eliot wrote John Blackwood: "I hope 'Clerical Scenes' are not being forgotten. I looked into them the other day, and felt that I had done nothing better than the writing in many parts of 'Janet.'" (*Letters, 3,* 267.) She may have been thinking of the expression she gives there to the doctrine of sympathy about which she felt so deeply. Or perhaps she felt that in the story she had done full justice to her girlhood religion, compensating in a sense for previous harshness. Certainly she could be well satisfied with the story on both these points. But if she read "Janet's Repentance" solely with an eye for artistic excellence, she was probably best pleased with her presentation of the Milby scene. From this the

---

7. "Novelist-Philosophers: XII—George Eliot," *Horizon,* 17 (January 1948), 51.

story derives the truth which she considered it the aim of art to supply.

In "Janet's Repentance," George Eliot makes her first attempt at presenting a social setting which is an integral part of the problem posed by the action of the story. In comparison with that of *The Mill on the Floss* and *Middlemarch,* the action with which she is here concerned is lacking in depth and complexity, but her treatment of the Milby background gives a significant indication of the artistic method which enabled George Eliot to give St. Oggs and Middlemarch a reality beyond that of physical and geographical existence.

5. AFTERWORD: *SCENES OF CLERICAL LIFE* AND THE LATER NOVELS

Shortly after George Eliot's death, her friend W. M. W. Call wrote of *Scenes of Clerical Life:* "All the characteristic properties of George Eliot's literary genius appear in these volumes. . . . In them lies the substance of the thought, the promise of the power afterwards so splendidly exhibited in the greater works."[1] One should perhaps make the qualification "in rudimentary form" to dispel the suggestion that there was no development in her art, but in essence, the proposition is true. It is not surprising that it should be so, for George Eliot began to write fiction comparatively late in life, in the full strength of intellectual maturity, and with a great deal of experience as a literary critic behind her.

Some of the most important aspects of George Eliot's later work foreshadowed in the *Scenes* have been dealt with in detail in earlier parts of this study: her sympathy with human suffering, her tolerance of human limitations, and her unwavering insistence on the importance of commonplace men and women. Others, which are of less substantial significance in this first work, have been treated somewhat less fully: her concern with environment,

1. "George Eliot: Her Life and Writings," *WR*, N. S. 60 (July 1881), 165–67.

the distinctive turn of her humor, and her interest in the psychological aspects of personality. There are still others, however, and in these concluding paragraphs I shall discuss what seem to me the most important of them.

Much has been written about the operations of Nemesis in George Eliot's novels,[2] and not without reason, for the concept enters significantly into all her work. Perhaps no passage in her writings is more often quoted than Mr. Irwine's words in *Adam Bede:* " 'Consequences are unpitying. Our deeds carry terrible consequences, quite apart from any fluctuations that went before —consequences that are hardly ever confined to ourselves.' " (Chapter 16.) This is the primary moral law in the world of George Eliot's books, and her conception of this force in human lives is expressed both directly and indirectly in the *Scenes.* The operation of the doctrine is implied in "Amos Barton," where Amos' foolish and selfish behavior with regard to the Countess results in the death of Milly. It is clear from his words at Milly's grave that Amos feels himself justly punished for his past sins: " 'Milly, Milly, dost thou hear me? I didn't love thee enough—I wasn't tender enough to thee—but I think of it all now.' " (Chapter 10.) The doctrine is also implicit in the action of "Mr. Gilfil's Love Story," where Captain Wybrow's selfishness and dishonesty and Caterina's willful passion work themselves out in sorrow and suffering for all concerned. Nemesis looms large in the case of Sir Christopher Cheverel who, to spite his elder sister, had gone to great trouble and expense to break the entail on Cheverel Manor and make Wybrow his heir. Wybrow's death, Sir Christopher feels, is retribution for his own pride and spitefulness: " 'Perhaps I've been wrong in not forgiving my sister,' " he reflects. " 'She lost one of *her* sons a little while ago. I've been too proud

2. See, for instance, V. R[endell], "George Eliot and the Classics: Greek and Nemesis," *Notes and Queries,* 192 (1947), 544, 546, 564–65.

and obstinate.' " (Chapter 18.) The idea of Nemesis is stated most explicitly of all in "Janet's Repentance." As Dempster falls deeper and deeper into moral deterioration, it is noted that "Nemesis is lame, but she is of colossal stature, like the gods; and sometimes, while her sword is not yet unsheathed, she stretches out her huge left arm and grasps her victim. The mighty hand is invisible, but the victim totters under the dire clutch." (Chapter 13.)

Notice is taken in this early story, as so frequently in George Eliot's later work, of that part of the larger idea of Nemesis which has to do with the apparent insignificance, even triviality, of the events which, through the complexities of human relationships, result in sorrow and suffering. In one way or another all of George Eliot's books emphasize the inextricability of men's lives—" 'Men's lives are as thoroughly blended with each other as the air they breathe: evil spreads as necessarily as disease,' " says Mr. Irwine in *Adam Bede* (Chapter 41)—and our inability to foresee ends in beginnings. At one point in "Janet's Repentance" the narrator observes, "The seeds of things are very small" (Chapter 13); and Mr. Tryan tells Janet, " 'We cannot foretell the working of the smallest event in our own lot.' " (Chapter 18.) Such statements point forward to the far-reaching consequences of Arthur Donnithorne's light-hearted flirtation, to the Tulliver and Transome family histories, to the complicated fabric of life in Middlemarch. The stern doctrine of consequences stated specifically early in "Janet's Repentance"—"We reap what we sow" (Chapter 5)— and previously exemplified in Amos Barton and Sir Christopher Cheverel, is illustrated again and again in George Eliot's books. "Our deeds determine us, as much as we determine our deeds," she writes in *Adam Bede* (Chapter 29); as motto to a crucial chapter in *Middlemarch* she sets the words:

Our deeds still travel with us from afar,
And what we have been makes us what we are. (Chapter 70.)

In *Felix Holt* she quotes Aeschylus:

> 'Tis law as steadfast as the throne of Zeus—
> Our days are heritors of days gone by.[3]

Particular characters whose histories illustrate these ideas come readily to mind—Arthur Donnithorne and Hetty Sorrel, Maggie and Tom Tulliver, Godfrey Cass, Mrs. Transome, Tito Melema, Lydgate, Bulstrode, and Gwendolen Harleth, to name some of the most important.

It should be noted that in "Janet's Repentance" the austere concept of Nemesis is tempered somewhat. Possibly because she was primarily concerned here with regeneration rather than deterioration, George Eliot suggests that though the operation of the law of consequences is inexorable, it is not invariably retributive; or to put it another way, the seeds of good must come to harvest as surely as the seeds of evil. This seems to be the thought in the following passage concerning Janet's mother:

> She tried to have hope and trust, though it was hard to believe that the future would be anything else than the harvest of the seed that was being sown before her eyes. But always there is seed being sown silently and unseen, and everywhere there come sweet flowers without our foresight or labour. We reap what we sow, but Nature has love over and above that justice, and gives us shadow and blossom and fruit that spring from no planting of ours. (Chapter 5.)

Despite the uncharacteristic sentimentality of this qualification of the doctrine of consequences—a concession to the sentimental ending of the story perhaps—the justice of the doctrine is accepted,

---

3. Motto to Chap. 48. In the article cited above, Rendell notes that George Eliot emphasized the idea of Nemesis by "alterations the Greek does not justify." The second line, he writes, should be rendered: "That the doer should suffer: it is ordinance." See *Notes and Queries*, 192 (1947), 545.

and its operation, though in some measure offset, is not called into question.[4]

Another factor connecting *Scenes of Clerical Life* and the later work is the appearance in the *Scenes* of certain situations and relationships to which George Eliot will return repeatedly. It is often remarked that her heroines tend to fall in love with men who are not worthy of them, and there is ample support for the statement. The characters of her first fiction provide an early demonstration of this unhappy situation. Milly and the stupid Amos, Caterina and the selfish Wybrow, Janet and the brutal Dempster—all bear witness to George Eliot's propensity for portraying mismatched men and women. It has been suggested that she gave her heroines the beauty which she did not herself possess and then proceeded to punish them for having it; or that in punishing them she punished herself, relieving the sense of guilt that she is supposed to have felt about her irregular union with Lewes.[5] The evidence of George Eliot's life and letters, however, in large part invalidates such suggestions, and one is more inclined to feel that her interest in such situations is due not to a cruel or neurotic impulse, but to the fact that they offer the best field for exercising her powers of moral analysis and provide interesting material for her dramas of egoism and self-deception.

Mary H. Deakin has pointed out another element in the *Scenes* which is significant as a foreshadowing of later work. "Janet's

4. Of this passage Bourl'honne says: "G. Eliot reconnaît cependant qu'il y a une sorte de générosité dans la Nature qui, parfois, permet à l'homme d'échapper aux conséquences logiques de ses actes. . . . Mais G. Eliot n'a pas trouvé dans cette idée une source véritable d'inspiration, et elle ne l'a pas intégrée dans le système général de sa pensée, qui est restée dominée par l'idée de la nécessité." (*George Eliot, Essai de biographie intellectuelle et morale, 1819–1854* [Paris, 1933], p. 136n.)

5. For one statement of this view, see Anne Fremantle, *George Eliot* (New York, 1933), pp. 87–88. Bourl'honne writes: "Nous croyons que son oeuvre est inspirée d'un sentiment de réparation par rapport à sa vie." (*George Eliot*, p. 191.)

Repentance," she observes, "is of importance also as containing a study of a relation which always interested George Eliot—a noble womanly nature, touched with some faults or some weakness . . . looking eagerly for guidance and comfort to a man of about her own age."[6] In this connection Miss Deakin mentions Esther Lyon and Felix Holt, Dorothea Brooke and Ladislaw, and Gwendolen Harleth and Daniel Deronda. To a lesser extent Maggie Tulliver and Philip Waken and Caterina and Mr. Gilfil also exemplify the theme. The treatment of this relationship in "Janet's Repentance," like that of the noble woman and less worthy man mentioned above, is significant mainly in that it provides a yardstick with which to measure the growing subtlety and strength of George Eliot's art. There is also, however, a biographical interest in her preoccupation with the theme. Miss Deakin is probably correct in observing that it reflects a deep need in George Eliot's own personality—"she loved to picture that healing, comforting reception of wise teaching which she in her youth had craved so strongly and often so vainly."[7]

In the light of George Eliot's later work, *Scenes of Clerical Life* is of most interest stylistically for the use of scientific illustration in the stories. This characteristic was remarked from the first. Concerning "Amos Barton," John Blackwood wrote George Eliot in January 1857 that a friend of his, W. G. Hamley, thought "the Author very possibly a *man of Science,*" adding that "the idea . . . had occurred to me before from some of the illustrations." (*Letters, 2,* 291.) The following phrases will show what the publisher had in mind: "as necessary a 'condition of thought' as Time and Space"; "the mental retina"; "the plenum of his own brain"; "the delicate visitation of atoms" (of an odor); "an amalgam of dissimilar ingredients"; "the quivering life in the water-drop"; "a nucleus of healthy life in an organ hardening by disease"; "that idea of duty . . . which is to the moral life what the addition of a

6. *The Early Life of George Eliot* (Manchester, 1913), p. 135.
7. Ibid., p. 135.

great central ganglion is to animal life"; "subtle nerve filaments, which elude scientific lenses." Taken as they are out of context, these examples simply show George Eliot's use of particular scientific terms; in context, they illustrate in a broader way her manner of employing metaphor to convey precise meaning. Considering the circle in which George Eliot's life in London had been spent, it is not surprising that her creative impulse would turn so readily to the realm of science for its vocabulary. But it would be a mistake to think that the scientific element in her writing was the result of Lewes' influence or a reflection of anything other than her own interests and predilections. The strongest proof of this is to be found in the few short essays, semi-fictional in character, which she wrote for the *Coventry Herald* in 1846, several years before the move to London. Here and there in these papers, one sees plainly prefigured the scientific manner of illustration so noticeable to first readers of the *Scenes*. In one of the essays, "From the Note-book of an Eccentric," she says of a man's character that "it contained elements which would too probably operate as non-conductors, interposed between his highly charged mind and the negatively electrified souls around him."[8] In another she speaks of "the good, the true, the beautiful, which outlive every generation and are all-pervading as the light which vibrates from the remotest nebula to our own sun."[9] Like all artists, George Eliot drew her metaphors from the areas of knowledge and experience which engaged her imagination most strongly; given her cast of mind, she naturally turned often to science, not surprising for a mid-nineteenth-century intellectual.

Aside from the use of particular scientific terms, George Eliot's style in the *Scenes* might be termed scientific in the broader sense that the writing abounds in concrete illustration of all sorts, showing a scrupulous regard for clarity and precision. Blackwood perhaps used the word in this sense also. In reply to his comment,

8. *Early Essays* (privately printed, 1919), p. 16.
9. "How to Avoid Disappointment," *Early Essays*, p. 27.

George Eliot wrote: "I suppose my scientific illustrations must be a fault, since they seem to have obtruded themselves disagreeably on one of my readers." (*Letters, 2, 292.*) To which the publisher replied: "In regard to scientific illustrations neither Hamley nor I meant that you used them too much. We merely alluded to a sort of precision of expression or illustration which gave us the idea that the writer was accustomed to scientific definitions." (*Letters, 2, 293–94.*) This is the sense in which George Eliot's style throughout her career may be called scientific; it is interesting, in view of the common criticism of her later books, to find the scientific manner so much in evidence in her first work.

In *The Mill on the Floss,* describing Tom Tulliver's first return home from school, George Eliot writes of

> the happiness of passing from the cold air to the warmth and the kisses and the smiles of that familiar hearth, where the pattern of the rug and the grate and the fire-irons were "first ideas" that it was no more possible to criticise than the solidity and extension of matter. (Book II, Ch. 1.)

The comment serves very well to introduce a final aspect of the relationship between the *Scenes* and the later work. It is an aspect to be discussed in terms of George Eliot's personal psychology and circumstances, and it may be generally suggested by the word "nostalgia." The lines which follow those quoted above are significant in this connection:

> There is no sense of ease like the ease we felt in those scenes where we were born, where objects became dear to us before we had known the labour of choice, and where the outer world seemed only an extension of our own personality. . . . Very commonplace, even ugly, that furniture of our early home might look if it were put up to auction; an improved taste in upholstery scorns it; and is not the striving after something better and better in our surroundings, the grand char-

acteristic that distinguishes man from brute? . . . But heaven knows where that striving might lead us, if our affections had not a trick of twining round those old inferior things—if the loves and sanctities of our life had no deep immovable roots in memory.

George Eliot had known "the labour of choice"; all her moral and intellectual decisions from the Coventry days onward represent a "striving after something better and better." In making the choices which determined her emotional and intellectual existence, she was governed by a rigorous honesty which made it impossible for her to do otherwise than she did; yet the great change which these choices entailed could not be made without a painful sense of having cut herself off from a past she loved deeply. Her comfort lay in looking back. Looking back was more than a solace, however; it was a necessary factor in her understanding of herself and a safeguard against intellectual sterility. On this point Basil Willey has written with understanding and insight:

> As with Wordsworth, whom she greatly reverenced and in some ways resembled, the heart of her was kept alive by the recollection of her early life, and of the scenes and people associated with the feelings of childhood. In a sense her early novels are her *Prelude,* that is, the means by which she pierced below the hard crust formed by the years of translating, reviewing and mental overforcing, to the quickening beds of heartfelt memory which lay beneath. Having achieved this recovery of time past, she was then able to see in truer perspective the relations between advancing intellect and backward-yearning affections.[1]

The geological metaphor is appropriate. In 1859, George Eliot wrote to her friend Mme. Bodichon: "At present my mind works with the most freedom and the keenest sense of poetry in my

1. *Nineteenth Century Studies,* p. 205.

remotest past, and there are many strata to be worked through before I can begin to use *artistically* any material I may gather in the present." (*Letters, 3,* 128–29.) Thus, beginning in the *Scenes* and continuing through *Adam Bede, The Mill on the Floss,* and *Silas Marner,* George Eliot, in the warmth of old affection, explores the "deep immovable roots" of her life. Willey's reference to the "recovery of time past," inevitably suggesting Proust, is appropriate, too, for if the early books are her *Prelude* they are also her "recherche du temps perdu."[2] "It is not surprising," she writes at the beginning of "Amos Barton," "that I recall with a fond sadness Shepperton Church as it was in the old days." In the process of recalling—not just Shepperton Church but the whole tenor of Midland life as she had known it before she had known the "labour of choice"—she gained perspective and reassurance. "We understand how it was that her first book was *Scenes of Clerical Life,* and not *Middlemarch,*" Virginia Woolf observes.[3] It is unlikely that there was any choice in the matter—probably George Eliot could not have written *Middlemarch* had she not first written the *Scenes* and the other books of recollection, for surely the depth and power of *Middlemarch* would have been beyond the reach of a mind troubled or unsure of itself, a mind lacking the balance which George Eliot achieved through her successful "recovery of time past."

In the course of this study I have considered George Eliot's first work as an embodiment of her theory of fiction, as an expression

2. Proust's admiration for George Eliot, incidentally, is well known. In 1910 he wrote: "Il n'y a pas de littérature qui ait sur moi un pouvoir comparable à la littérature anglaise ou américaine. L'Allemagne, l'Italie, bien souvent la France, me laissent indifférent. Mais deux pages du *Moulin sur la Floss* me font pleurer." (Letter to Robert de Billy, quoted in *Hommage à Marcel Proust* [Paris, 1927], p. 32.) See also L. A. Bisson, "Proust, Bergson, and George Eliot," *Modern Language Review,* 40 (1945), pp. 104–14; and Franklin Gary "In Search of George Eliot: An Approach through Marcel Proust," *Symposium,* 4 (April 1933), 182–206.

3. *The Common Reader* (London, 1925), p. 209.

of her moral philosophy, and as a trying out of her narrative technique—all matters of interest to the student of literature. But the *Scenes* were not written for students and critics, and I should like in closing to speak briefly of them as a common reader—"uncorrupted by literary prejudices," as Dr. Johnson prescribes, and without "the refinements of subtility and the dogmatism of learning." While the student is first interested in the *Scenes* because of their authorship, the common reader will be interested or not, will re-read them or not, simply for what the stories themselves offer. What would they offer, one might ask, to a reader innocent of literary history who came upon them in all the lifeless anonymity of old bound volumes of *Blackwood's?* Two things, I think: an intimate acquaintance with people who are worth knowing, and the pleasure of entering a world which refreshes us with its differences from our own. A few of the major characters—Milly Barton, old Mr. Gilfil, Janet—and almost all the background figures give us that sense of extending our own identities which is one of the prime pleasures of reading. It is not so much that we learn from these people; rather, as in life, we simply enjoy a companionship with them. Our existence is richer for the knowledge that whatever may happen in our world, we can go back to Cross Farm, to Shepperton vicarage, even to Milby, and find there people who reawaken in us the sense of life's variety.

Inextricably related to our pleasure in these people is the charm of their world, a charm depending always upon our sense of the reality of the place. This qualification is important, for the world of the *Scenes* is not always charming in itself—the charm lies in our sense of its reality. Ultimately, however, our pleasure derives not from the people and places presented to us, but from the suffusion into this world of George Eliot's own sympathy and affection. A lesser writer than Goldsmith could have made Wakefield charming; Milby and Shepperton need George Eliot. It is, as Leslie Stephen noted long ago, "the sympathetic appreciation of the old-fashioned life by a large intellect" that gives *Scenes of*

Clerical Life a "singular charm."[4] Virginia Woolf, amplifying her father's thought, speaks of the pleasures of "basking in the light and sunshine of *Scenes of Clerical Life,* feeling the large mature mind spreading itself with a luxurious sense of freedom in the world of her 'remotest past.' "[5] Mrs. Woolf, with her own fine sense of the past and her sensitivity to impressions which are very hard to describe on paper, was better able than most people to define the charm of George Eliot's early work. It is not inappropriate, therefore, to conclude this study with the words of one who not only understood the problems of the novelist's art but who also made the common reader's point of view particularly her own:

> The beauty of those first books, *Scenes of Clerical Life, Adam Bede, The Mill on the Floss,* is very great. It is impossible to estimate the merit of the Poysers, the Gilfils, the Bartons, and the rest with all their surroundings and dependencies, because they have put on flesh and blood and we move among them, now bored now sympathetic, but always with the unquestioning acceptance of all that they say and do, which we accord to the great originals only. The flood of memory and humour which she pours so spontaneously into one figure, one scene after another, until the whole fabric of ancient rural England is revived, has so much in common with a natural process that it leaves us with little consciousness that there is anything to criticise. We accept; we feel the delicious warmth and release of spirit which the great creative writers alone procure for us. As one comes back to the books after years of absence they pour out, even against our expectation, the same store of energy and heat, so that we want more than anything to idle in the warmth as in the sun beating down from the red orchard wall.[6]

4. "Cross, Mary Ann," *Dictionary of National Biography* (1888), *13,* 219.
5. *The Common Reader,* p. 210.
6. Ibid., p. 211.

INDEX

Index

185; on realism, 37; on GE, 42, 94, 146, 151. *See also* under individual stories
Liggins, Joseph, 13 n.
Literary Gazette, 21–22 n.
London Times, 20–21
Lucas, Samuel, 20–21

McCarthy, Justin, 165 n.–66n.
Mackenzie, Henry, 59
MacLean, Kenneth, 59 n.
Maurice, F. D., 62, 64
May, J. Lewis, 103 n., 145
Meredith, George, 103
Middlemarch, 68, 103, 176; and *Scenes,* 130, 188
Miles, William, 175
Mill, J. S., 61–62
Mill on the Floss, The, 43–44, 186–88, 190; and *Scenes,* 130, 134
"Mr. Gilfil's Love Story," 5, 7–8, 19–20, 22, 24 n., 25, 41–42, 180, 183, 189; background of, 11–13, 15; Blackwood on, 40–41, 43–45, 144; GE on, 45; and doctrine of sympathy, 72–77, 81; and "Amos Barton," 122–23, 125; labored writing of, 125–30, 133, 146; as romance, 125, 130–35, 139–40, 143; sentimentality of, 136–40; as melodrama, 140–44; critical opinion of, 144–46
Mudge, I. G., 9 n.
Mulock, Dinah, 17. *See also* Craik, Mrs. George

National Review, 16–17, 21
"Natural History of German Life, The," 28–29
Newdigate family, 11–13
Niebuhr, Richard, 90

Ogilvie, John, 58
Olcott, Charles S., 9 n.

Overton, J. H., 166 n.

Proust, Marcel, 188 n.

Quarterly Review, 128

Reade, Charles, 17–18
Rendell, V., 180 n., 182 n.
Revue des deux mondes, 21–22 n.
Riehl, W. H., 28, 35, 37, 96 n.
Rousseau, J. J., 61
Ruskin, John, 23, 29, 36–37 n.; on Victorian home, 106–07; on Dickens, 111
Russell, G. W. E., 170 n.

"Sad Fortunes of the Reverend Amos Barton, The," 2–5, 7, 19, 22, 25, 28, 33, 49, 180, 183, 189; background of, 9–11, 14–15; GE on, 38–39; Blackwood on, 40, 46–47, 51 n., 115–16, 122; and doctrine of sympathy, 65–73, 75–77; humor of, 93–103; Lewes on, 103–04; pathos of, 103–22
Saturday Review, 18–20, 27 n.
Scenes of Clerical Life. See under individual stories
Scott, Walter, 29, 41
Sears, M. E., 9 n.
Shaftesbury, 3d Earl of, 57–58
Shelley, Percy Bysshe, 60
Shilton, Sally, 12
Sibree, Jr., John, 6 n., 52
Sikes, Thomas, 174
Silas Marner, 188; and *Scenes,* 98
"Silly Novels by Lady Novelists," 33–35, 147
Smith, Adam, 58–60
Smith, Albert, 22, 110
Stang, Richard, 28 n.
Statesman, 21
Stephen, Leslie, 68, 144–45, 189–90
Sterling, John, 62

Index

Sterne, Laurence, 59
Stewart, Dugald, 58
Swayne, G. C., Rev., 22

Tennyson, Alfred, Lord, 23, 64
Thackeray, William Makepeace, 16–17, 22–23, 41, 49, 50, 67 n., 118
Tillotson, Kathleen, 109–10, 148 n.
Trollope, Anthony, 16–17, 41, 102–03

Waugh, Evelyn, 109–10
Westminster Review, 4, 27–39 passim, 147–50, 158
Willey, Başil, 53, 56, 77, 158, 187–88
Woolf, Virginia, 188, 190
Wordsworth, William, 29, 37 n., 53, 59, 60–61, 89, 187

Yonge, Charlotte Mary, 17, 118 n.
Young, Edward, 32